CRYSTAL PALACE F.C.

1969-1990
A BIASED COMMENTARY

Written and illustrated by Chris Winter

RED POST PRESS

First edition published in 1990 by

Red Post Press
39a Red Post Hill
London SE24 9JJ

ISBN 0 9516636 0 7

Contents

Dedicated
to
Len

Introduction

The first game of football I ever went to was Crystal Palace against Carlisle, in the Second Division in 1968. I doubt if I had heard of Palace, but like any other ten-year-old I knew all the big names of the day, players like George Best and Bobby Charlton, and had seen and loved the film of England winning the World Cup at Wembley. Everyone else at the time said they supported either Manchester United or Chelsea, but from that distant Saturday afternoon onwards one of my few certainties has been that I am a Palace fan.

It probably helped that the score that day was 5-0, but what hooked me was the atmosphere of the crowd, unlike anything I had known before, and the fact that everyone there was having fun. Best of all was the moment when "Glad All Over" came on the tannoy, and all around the ground hands stretched out and pounded the advertising boards in unison ; I soon joined in.

My purpose in writing this book is not to produce a definitive statistical record - for that I would recommend 'The Crystal Palace Story" by Roy Peskett and the recent book by Mike Purkiss - but rather to set down my own subjective memories of the last 21 years, and my opinions of the characters involved. Some of what I have written you will agree with, but most of it you probably won't, since we all see the game in different ways, but I simply hope that you will recognize the sentiments that lie behind what amounts to a labour of love.

As well as covering the events of each season from 1969 – Palace's first ever in Division One – to 1990, when we nearly won the F.A.Cup at Wembley, I have also chosen an imaginary team from everyone who has played for Palace during that time. I give my thoughts on the best players in each position in the final chapters, but for quick reference the team is as follows:

JOHN JACKSON
PETER WALL
KEN SANSOM
STEVE KEMBER
JOHN McCORMICK
IAN EVANS
DON ROGERS
GEOFF THOMAS
DAVE SWINDLEHURST
IAN WRIGHT
VINCE HILAIRE

Finally, thanks are due to Keith Andrews, Roger Dickson and Ian Weller and to my wife, Barbara, for their invaluable help with the production of this tribute, and to all the players who I have so enjoyed watching and moaning about.

1969-70

The traditional response of a newly promoted club is to go out and buy a couple of players with First Division experience to help to dig in, but Palace's immediate concern was the building of a new stand at breakneck speed, where once had been a dangerous mound of earth. As a tribute to his own efforts, this was called, with the degree of modesty expected of the Chairman, the 'Arthur Wait Stand'.

ARTHUR WAIT

Bert Head, as was his habit, went to Scotland to sign three new players, Roger Hynd, Gerry Queen and Per Bartram, and also bought Alan Pinkney from Exeter City. Queen was intended to be a direct replacement for Bobby Woodruff as centre forward, and Hynd was to accompany John McCormick in central defence, allowing Mel Blyth more of a midfield role. Apart from these two changes, it was essentially the same team that had won promotion who lined up for Palace's first ever game in the First Division, against no less a side than the waning Manchester United. After finishing 11th. in the league the previous season, Matt Busby had handed over team affairs to the ill-fated Wilf McGuiness, and the team for his first game in charge was still packed with household names, the front line consisting of Willie Morgan, Brian Kidd, Bobby Charlton, Denis Law and George Best. Although still a glamorous side, it is clear in retrospect that by

this time United's best days were behind them. However, it was still an achievement for a mostly unmodified Second Division team such as Palace to earn a 2-2 draw in front of a record breaking crowd of 48,610, after twice going ahead with goals from Mel Blyth and, on his debut, Gerry Queen. A comfortable home victory against Sunderland and a good performance at Everton, despite losing 2-1, seemed to suggest that Palace might be reasonably comfortable in such company, and at least defensively they were looking fairly capable.

The pattern for the season began to emerge in the next game, however, when the opponents were again Sunderland – destined for relegation that season – this time at Roker Park. Just a week after beating them 2-0, Palace concentrated on earning an away point, and despite never being troubled by an attack that had so far failed to score in four games, were content to come away with a goalless draw. Bobby Woodruff was back in the side in place

GERRY QUEEN

of the injured Gerry Queen, and the Dane Per Bartram came on as substitute for Cliff Jackson; the fact that these four strikers only managed 17 goals between them all season explains why Palace struggled to survive. Jackson and Woodruff were clearly nearing the end of their careers, and this was to be the last season in

Division One for each of them. Gerry Queen, although not without both skill and speed, appeared to be typical of the old fashioned inside forward, and would have benefitted

MARK LAZARUS

from playing alongside someone with a bit more muscle, while Bartram, the Danish international intended to fill that role, had problems initially with his work permit, being classified as an alien, and having to report regularly to the police! When he did come into the team, he proved a disappointment, and only played a few games before returning to Morton the following season.

Hence, although Palace were able to achieve a good number of draws against good sides, they only managed five more victories all season, albeit with two of them being against recent champions Manchester City. The defence was still being held together by the good form of McCormick, and the heroics of John Jackson in goal, and Kember was superb in midfield, but nothing too much was happening up front. The year 1969 ended with an appalling run of 10 games during which Palace won only three points, scoring six goals and conceding 23, and bracketed by 5-1 home defeats at the hands of Arsenal, at the start of November, and Chelsea on Boxing Day, when the crowd of 49,498 set another new record. The team selection became even more cautious, with Woodruff and Lazarus

departing for Cardiff and Orient respectively, and Phil Hoadley coming into the side together with the reliable David Payne. With injuries to Tony Taylor, Roger Hoy and Cliff Jackson, Bert Head was also forced to use reserve players such as Trevor Dawkins and Len Tomkins, and Palace went into the new year third from bottom, above Sunderland and Sheffield Wednesday, but still looking certainties for relegation. A 3-2 defeat at West Bromwich Albion in the new year left them in the bottom two and surely doomed.

Things began to look up, however, when Bert Head persuaded Bobby Tambling, one of Chelsea's greatest ever goalscorers, to come to Selhurst on loan for 3 games. Then, after unsuccessfully pursuing several forwards, including Jimmy Greaves, he signed the Scottish International Jim Scott from

JIM SCOTT

Newcastle. Although he failed to score in his first 11 games, Scott's inclusion alongside Tony Taylor balanced the forward line, and Palace began to look more of a team as they forced valuable draws at St.James' Park, Old Trafford and Molineux, three of the most intimidating grounds for away teams. They also managed two wins in a row for the only time all season, when they beat both Manchester City and Southampton in the space of four days. The most notable achievement during this period, however, was the victory over Spurs in the F.A.Cup 4th round. After holding them 0-0 at White Hart Lane, Palace won the replay the following Wednesday night against a side which contained seven full international players, including Greaves, Alan Gilzean and Alan Mullery, as well as a youngster in his first season, Steve Perryman. Although Spurs, along

TONY TAYLOR

with Arsenal and Manchester United, were to finish only in a middle of the table position at the end of that season, they were still one of the best sides around, and Palace fully deserved to win what remains the best Cup Tie seen at Selhurst Park, with a goal from Gerry Queen, and the usual flat out performance from Roger Hoy. Somehow, after that, it seemed inevitable that Palace would stay up, and despite going out of the Cup to Chelsea, and losing a crucial 'four-pointer' at home to Sheffield Wednesday, they completed the season by beating Manchester City again, the only double that year. Palace eventually escaped relegation by just a single point, an outcome that had seemed most improbable at the turn of the year.

A significant factor in Palace's survival was the form of Mel Blyth, who deposed Roger Hynd as John McCormick's partner in central defence, creating a combination that was to last for the next two and a half seasons. The

most worrying thing, though, was that the team had clearly not progressed since winning promotion, and of the new players, Hynd had added nothing, Bartram and Pinkney had failed to make any impression, whilst Queen found himself rather isolated up front. The core of the team which had come up were still playing well enough, namely John Jackson, McCormick and Kember, but unlike fellow newcomers Derby County, their natural home looked to be the Second Division.

Despite some poor football on the pitch, the club was fairly successful at cultivating a friendly atmosphere and a feeling of homeliness in the days before the segregation of rival fans, and the Whitehorse Lane end, with supporters of both teams mixing quite happily, became the natural area for young fans to stand, without having to be designated as such. That this no longer happens at football grounds is the greatest shame of all, and one thing for which one can be forgiven a nostalgic view. Unfortunately, what too many people now become misty-eyed about is the passing of the great players and the great teams, which implies that the game has become inferior. I have never been convinced by the protestations of such as George Best and Rodney Marsh that there aren't the "characters" now that there were in the 60's and 70's. In reality, such players stood out as exceptions at the time, and although few would deny that Best was certainly a wonderful player, to my mind he forgives his own misdemeanours too readily. Every team, in most seasons, will have players who stand out, but they are generally of no use unless they are concerned as much with the team as with themselves.

1970-71

It was clear from the previous season that Bert Head would have to spend some money on a good centre forward, and the man he went for was Chelsea's Alan Birchenall, rated at £100,000, who came in a package with Bobby Tambling. The other significant purchase was that of Peter Wall from Liverpool, who immediately consigned left back John Loughlan to the reserves. With Birchenall's arrival, there was no place for Cliff Jackson, and he returned to the West Country, with Torquay. Mel Blyth's good run at the end of the previous season and the maturing of Phil Hoadley also meant that Roger Hynd was no longer needed, and he moved on to Birmingham. Perhaps more surprising was the loss of the very adaptable Roger Hoy to Luton.

BOBBY TAMBLING

Before a ball had been kicked, the newspapers had front page stories about Palace's new wages and bonus scheme, which gave rise to speculation that their players could become the game's highest earners, with up to £300 in their weekly pay packet! Whatever the true figures, Palace made a tremendous start to the new season, and after four wins and three draws in the first eight games found themselves sitting third in the league, behind Leeds United and Manchester City, a high point from which the slide was to be relentless. However, at this

point the team were earning some deserved praise for the quality of their football, and the close-season signings were proving to be good ones. Alan Birchenall was exactly the kind of partner that Gerry Queen needed, and for the first part of the season at least the combination of Tambling's attacking instincts on the wing, Birchenall's strength in the air and Gerry Queen's speed proved quite effective, if not prolific.

Just as important was the extra dimension to Palace's defensive thinking added by left back Peter Wall. Although not a regular first team choice at Liverpool, some of that club's class had rubbed off on him, and he impressed as a cool, skilful player with the confidence to play the ball out of defence, and a touch of arrogance which could inspire his colleagues.

It appeared that Bert Head had transformed last season's no-hopers into a genuine First Division side by adding just three players, and although the core of the side remained intact, they were at this stage all playing to their limits. In October of 1970, after consecutive victories against Southampton and West Bromwich Albion at home, and by a single goal at Old Trafford to spoil Bobby Charlton's 500th game for United, the top six of the first division contained four London clubs – Arsenal, Spurs, Palace and Chelsea – along with Leeds and Manchester City, and for the first time Palace fans felt they really did belong in the elite. Confirmation that Palace's league position was no fluke came when they faced Arsenal in the 4th round of the League Cup. The Gunners were to win the F.A.Cup and League double that season, so it was a great feat for Palace, after forcing a 0-0 draw at Selhurst Park, to win the replay at Highbury, albeit against the run of play, with goals from Gerry Queen and a Bobby Tambling penalty.

It looked as if things were going Palace's way, because this game came just two days after a memorable home match against Leeds United, at that time two points clear at the top of the table. Despite matching Leeds for most of the game, Palace were unable to break through the mean defence, and found themselves a goal down with less than a minute left, and heading for an undeserved defeat. When the ball fell loose to John Sewell inside his own half, it looked as if the captain too had given up all hope, for instead of trying to find a team mate up front, he simply clogged the ball upfield as hard as he could, to the groans of the home crowd. The ball dropped gently towards the

JOHN SEWELL

Leeds goal, where Gary Sprake, with nobody else within 30 yards of him, prepared to take the simplest of catches inside the left hand post. But Gary Sprake was not like other men, and his mind began to wander. One moment the ball was safely in his hands, and the next it was behind him, in the net. Sprake looked around, searching desperately for the strange force which had sucked the ball from his grasp, but there was no one but himself to blame. Those of the crowd who had left the ground a couple of minutes early had missed the finest moment of comedy they were ever likely to see at Selhurst Park, but luckily for them - if not for the hapless goalkeeper - the slapstick was repeated on television every week until the end of the season. There is a photograph taken from behind the goal, which shows the keeper's

gloved hands firmly behind the ball as he catches it, and I imagine that among Gary Sprake's many nightmares, this one will always be one of the most frightening.

Although still on the heels of the leaders, the team was soon to be affected by injuries to Queen, Tambling and Payne, and the productive partnership of Birchenall and Queen was never able to recover its early promise. Jim Scott's form in place of Tambling was a dissappointment, and with Gerry Humphries and Trevor Dawkins pressed into service, a run of four games during December and January saw the team unable to score a single league goal, and knocked out of the F.A.Cup by Chelsea, always a particularly bitter pill to swallow. Things improved slightly after the purchase of an established goalscorer, Bolton's Terry Wharton, and home victories followed against Liverpool and Ipswich. The Liverpool result, with Gerry Queen scoring the only goal,

TERRY WHARTON

stood as Palace's first and only victory over them until a famous day nearly 20 years later. Thus, with two thirds of the season gone, Palace were still lying quite handy in 9th. position, with an outside chance still of qualifying for Europe, and everything to play for.

With the European possibilities in mind, a friendly game was arranged against the leaders of the Dutch League, PSV Eindhoven. It was certainly no disgrace to lose 4-2 against such a good side, but for some reason the effect on Palace was devastating. In the following eight games they only earned themselves one point, and after the home defeat by Coventry Bert Head allowed himself a rare public outburst when he claimed that several of his players were performing as if the season was over, which of course proved to be the case, only John Jackson escaping his wrath. One incident summed up the peculiar lack of passion in the team, when Alan Birchenall picked up a ball in the opponent's half of the field and, showing a good deal of skill, dribbled past several

league to a final, humiliating 6-0 defeat at Southampton was incomprehensible. The only consolation was that Palace finished in their highest ever league position, 18th. in the First Division, and comfortably clear of the two relegation places.

Some self respect was recovered after the season's end with good performances against Inter Milan and Cagliari in the Anglo-Italian Tournament, and the Palace fans, ever optimistic in the face of all the contradictory evidence, looked forward to next season in the knowledge that their team was now well and truly established in Division One.

ALAN BIRCHENALL

tackles as he looked in vain for a team mate sufficiently interested to receive a pass, eventually taking it all the way back to John Jackson in his own area.

After such a good start to the season, it was especially disappointing to witness such a decline, and it looked as though many of the players knew that they could achieve no more. John Sewell, certainly, was at the end of his career, and injury had affected John McCormick and David Payne, as well as Queen and Tambling, but the slide from third in the

1971-72

Bert Head obviously shared the fans' optimism, since no new players arrived during the summer, the only departure being that of John Sewell to Orient just before the start of the season. This brought about the conversion of David Payne from midfield to right back, which seemed a reasonable ploy since Payne had lost some speed, but had the experience to adapt well to a new role. Steve Kember, at the height of his powers, was the logical choice to take over as captain, and with this almost unchanged line up, Palace faced Newcastle in the first game of the season.

The major change that had taken place, though, was the introduction of a new playing strip – no doubt inspired by the pre-season efforts against Dutch opposition – consisting of two broad vertical bands of claret and blue on a white shirt. This was clearly based on the design used by Johann Cruyff's Ajax of Amsterdam, but instead of making the team look slick and Continental, it made the players look disturbingly lopsided. A conscious attempt had obviously been made to drag Palace's image into the modern era of the 70's, but the previous design of claret with thin light blue stripes was infinitely preferable. The previously spare and sophisticated programme underwent a radical change too, being superceded by surely one of the most unappealing designs in history. The cover featured an appalling drawing of an anonymous goalkeeper smiling feebly as the ball sails past him and into the net; patently not Jacko.

The game against Newcastle gave their new signing Malcolm McDonald his first chance in the First Division, but he was unable to bludgeon his way through a well organised Palace defence, and Steve Kember's brief career as captain began with a 2-0 victory. It was too early to assume that Palace could recover their excellent form of a year before, but the signs were good. The dramatic loss of form over the next eight games, then, is hard

to explain. The only answer I can offer is that too many of the players, those with years of experience as much as those who had won promotion two years earlier, felt that they had arrived as First Division regulars and had become complacent, with the result that Bert

BERT HEAD

Head was no longer able to motivate them. Over the next few weeks, as the team struggled to win just one point from eight games, it seemed that the harder they tried the worse they played, and the fans started to express their impatience more than they ever had before. Bearing in mind that the home gates were still averaging nearly 30,000, there is no doubt that they had a perfect right to expect a lot more for their money.

On the Sunday morning following a 3-0 defeat at Spurs, the board met and demanded that the manager should take decisive action to reverse the decline. Within a week, Bert Head had sold his two most valuable assets; Steve Kember to Chelsea for a record fee of £170,000, and Alan Birchenall to Leicester. The justification for this was that the money would be used to inject a new spirit into the team with the purchase of half a dozen new players, in a most dramatic shake-up of staff. Three others to have played their last games for Palace were Phil Hoadley, sold to Orient, the disappointing Jim Scott, and Terry Wharton. The fans, already critical of the sale of Kember in particular, were even more bemused when the new blood was announced. Each day the newspapers reported a new signing; the first was Bobby Kellard, familiar enough to most from his previous spell at the

BOBBY KELLARD

club, and a straightforward replacement for Steve Kember in midfield, but John Craven, Sammy Goodwin and Bobby Bell were far from household names. Indeed, Goodwin had been making a living as a car salesman while playing part-time for Airdrie! The final two newcomers, arriving a month later, sounded distinctly more exciting; the Celtic pair John Hughes and Willie Wallace, both forwards with Scottish International caps and European experience.

With the loss of Kember, John Jackson briefly became team captain, but by November this duty had passed to Bobby Kellard, one of the game's natural skippers. With so many new players thrown together at one time, it was something of a surprise to defeat Everton 2-1, the goal coming from a young and enthusiastic Ross Jenkins, playing only his fourth game in the first team. By the time of the home fixture with Sheffield United in December, results had started to improve, and Palace were playing

like a team again, albeit with a definite defensive bias. It must be remembered that Sheffield United were at this time lying near the top of the First Division, and after beating Ipswich 7-0, were being spoken of as a major new force in the game. The 5-1 victory that ensued was certainly the highlight of the entire season for Palace fans, and nobody who was there on that day, or who saw the highlights on television, will ever forget the two goals scored by John Hughes, who surprisingly only scored twice more in his 23 games for Palace. 'Yogi', as he had been known at Celtic, was so named because of his size and strength, and without ever having much speed, he had the ability to shake off defenders through sheer physical power, while keeping his head down and the

JOHN HUGHES

ball always under close control. There was something immediately likeable about him, and he became a hero overnight with his performance that day. His first goal was a gem in its own right, a diagonal solo run from the halfway line completed with a strong left foot shot to put Palace 2-0 up after only 7 minutes. It was his second goal, however, and Palace's fourth, which ensured his place in history. Picking the ball up on the left, following a free kick for yet another foul on him, he seemed to move in slow motion as he lumbered inside, dipping his shoulders to shrug off a couple of challenges before working his way into a position some 35 yards from goal. Without breaking stride he swung his massive right leg at the ball and produced a shot of such power and accuracy that it was in the net almost before the helpless goalkeeper could react. Palace's other scorers that day were Tony

WILLIE WALLACE

Taylor, John McCormick and Gerry Queen, and although Willie Wallace failed to complete a unique nap hand for the Scots, he also looked good on a day when everything went right for his new team.

As well as being a splendid performance, perhaps more important was the fact that the result lifted Palace off the bottom of the table, and in the process vindicated Bert Head's faith in his new players, and in particular his persistent policy of looking to Scotland for fresh blood. Unfortunately, Yogi Hughes was injured towards the end of that match, and only managed a further five games during the rest of the season. It was a season which turned out to be the usual hard slog to avoid relegation, which they did by once again finishing third from bottom, but clear by four points. Despite this struggle, the second half of the season kept the fans more interested than had been the case the previous year, and in the end survival was considered a fine

achievement after such a dreadful start. Of the new players, Bobby Kellard was an unqualified success, with the fighting spirit that had been so lacking the year before, and John Craven showed occasional bursts of skill which promised better to come.

This had been the year of a well publicised 'referee's clampdown', a good idea in theory, but turned into a farce by the inflexibility of the authorities. Referees, who will always be considered inconsistent if the rules allow for interpretation, were suddenly given strict instructions as to what constitutes foul play, and for a while defenders were unable to tackle from behind, however cleanly. Rather than trying to attract referees of a higher calibre, and with more natural authority, the league effectively took some of the responsibility away from them, and the result was confusion all round, for players were now finding themselves penalised for playing the way they had been doing for years. The overall effect, far from encouraging skilful football – as had been the intention – was that teams developed more efficient strategies for cheating, following the fine example set by the mighty Leeds United.

1972-73

Before the season began there was no end of transfer speculation in the press, although most of it was due to Palace having earned a reputation for throwing money around, and therefore being linked with every player going. There was no doubt, however, that a new centre forward was a priority, considering that the top scorer the previous season had been the ageing Bobby Tambling, with just 11 goals in all competitions. Of the other forwards, John Craven had done best with eight goals, but Queen and Wallace were clearly below par. Bert Head claimed that during the summer he had been pursuing a total of 22 players, and among those he was apparently on the verge of signing were Stan Bowles, Alan Gowling and Derek Johnson, as well as England regular Alan Mullery. Nevertheless, come the kick off, the only significant changes to the side

ALAN PINKNEY

were the inclusion of Alan Pinkney in place of Sammy Goodwin in midfield, and Ross Jenkins replacing Gerry Queen. The playing strip had been made even worse with the addition of a white stripe down the middle, and a new badge in a supposedly high-tech design.

The league, determined to further pursue the war on foul play announced a new penalty points system, which at least had the merit of

bringing some consistency to what had seemed fairly arbitrary refereeing the year before. Something I have yet to see anyone booked for is the offence, carrying one penalty point, of "A player using the shoulders of his own team colleague to assist in the heading of the ball", so this practice at least must have been successfuly stamped out.

Palace's start this time was not disastrous, although suggestive of yet another season spent in the bottom half of the table. With four draws and a defeat in the first five games, again the problem looked to be one of scoring goals, but perhaps the most worrying incident was the broken leg sustained by Peter Wall in the 1-1 draw against his old club, Liverpool. This was, in effect, the end of his season, and although he was loaned to Orient for rehabilitation once the break had mended, it was to be another two and a half years before he regained a regular place in the side. The left back position went at first to the 18 year old Bill Roffey, and then Tony Taylor was moved back from midfield to defence, fairly successfully. By now, just four years after promotion, the only five survivors from that team made up the entire defence; John Jackson, David Payne, Tony Taylor, John McCormick and Mel Blyth.

Following a single goal defeat of Manchester City, courtesy of an own goal and Jackson's penalty save from Francis Lee, came a 2-1 victory over Newcastle, and at the beginning of September Palace were sitting comfortably in 10th position, a significant improvement on the previous year. The Newcastle game featured a remarkable goal for Palace which, as it turned out, used up their quota of luck for the next two months. Willie Wallace lost control of the ball in the penalty area, but as he chased after it he stumbled into a defender, who could hardly believe it when the referee awarded a penalty. Although absolutely nobody agreed, the decision stood, and it was left to Palace's captain Bobby Kellard to take the spot kick. As he ran up, he slipped over and miskicked the ball completely with his left foot. This sent a clump of earth towards the goal, at the same time diverting the ball slowly into the net, with the goalkeeper McFaul utterly flummoxed.

The following Tuesday, a dire performance at home to Fourth Division Stockport County ended Palace's interest in the League Cup, and five straight league defeats sent them to the very bottom of the table. During this time, including two Texaco Cup games against Hearts, Palace went six games without scoring, and despite losing out to Manchester United for the signature of the £200,000 striker Ted MacDougall, Bert Head made it clear that he was about to make some big money signings. The weeks that followed echoed the shake-up of the previous autumn, with Palace's transfer record broken twice; first by Iain Philip, a 21-year-old costing £115,000 from Dundee, and then Don Rogers, coming from Swindon for

CHARLIE COOKE

£150,000. Paddy Mulligan and Charlie Cooke also joined from Chelsea, and with John McCormick being dropped in favour of Bobby Bell, half the team was changed in a stroke. With Mulligan immediately installed as captain, a disgruntled Bobby Kellard demanded a transfer and was soon dropped, as were Wallace, Tambling and Jenkins.

Before the arrival of Rogers, Palace were unlucky to lose 3-2 to Arsenal in a home game, with all three Arsenal goals considered highly dubious, and none more so than Charlie George's penalty. Paul Hammond, playing only his second game in goal in place of the

PAUL HAMMOND

injured Jackson, held on to the ball at the second attempt and seemed to have saved the penalty, but the referee considered that the ball had crossed the line, and Palace were denied a crucial point. Although the television evidence was inconclusive, it was one of those games where Palace certainly deserved a result which would have lifted them off the bottom of the First Division, but it was not until Don Rogers' arrival that there seemed any hope of a genuine revival. Rogers was already famous, having scored two goals for Swindon in the 1969 League Cup final against Arsenal, but the big clubs had remained unconvinced that he could step up in class, and consequently he had remained a star of the lower divisions until rejoining his old boss Bert Head at Palace. Any doubts about him were quickly dispelled in his first appearance, when he scored the goal against Everton which gave Palace only their third victory from 16 games. This goal was the first of many in exactly the same mould; racing onto a through ball from John Craven from his own half and beating the defender for speed before drawing the goalkeeper, looking up and placing the ball sweetly past him and into the net. Although he did score the odd scrambled goal, these solo efforts became his trademark, and as a crowd pleaser he was one of the best in the game. His heroic status was confirmed in the famous 5-0 defeat of Manchester United a few weeks later. This was the first game for another new signing, Alan Whittle from Everton, and he was to score a single goal alongside a brace each by Rogers and Paddy Mulligan. Arthur Wait described the losing team as "The worst United side I have ever seen", and it gave the board at Old Trafford the final excuse that they needed to get rid of their latest manager, Frank O'Farrell, and replace him with Tommy Docherty.

At last able to score goals, and augmented by the signing of Millwall's highest ever goalscorer, Derek Possee, Palace managed some good results which suggested the possibility of survival, but what the fans were unaware of at the time was that Bert Head's days were numbered. Ray Bloye, a front man for the business consortium Matthews

RAY BLOYE

Holdings, had been installed earlier in the season as vice-chairman, and despite his unconvincing protestations that "when I joined the club as a Director, I had neither the ambition nor the intention to become Chairman", by

November the old Chairman Arthur Wait had become 'Life President', and Bloye's firm were firmly in control. It was not until the following March that it was announced that Bert Head was to be kicked upstairs, becoming General Manager until the end of the season, but it had been planned for some time. At this stage Palace were still one place away from

JOHN CRAVEN

relegation, and it seems remarkable that Head wasn't allowed to see out the last few weeks of the season in charge, but Bloye clearly felt that he could buy instant success, and so Malcolm Allison arrived, heralded as the saviour of Crystal Palace.

In a touching show of loyalty, Bert Head and his assistant Terry Long introduced Allison to the crowd before the home game against Chelsea, and for an afternoon at least Palace could hail the new Messiah. The 2-0 victory over Chelsea was Palace's first against a London club in all their time in the First Division, and Jim Cannon had an outstanding debut in defence, marking Peter Osgood out of the game, and rushing upfield to head in the second goal. However, Palace were unable to win again until the last game of the season at Manchester City, and despite achieving a better points total than in either 1971 or 1972, relegation finally became reality after four seasons of almost constant struggle.

1973-74

Malcolm Allison wanted to save not only Crystal Palace, but English football, yet he will be remembered mostly for what is called 'flamboyance' – his big cigar, big hat and a big mouth. It was a surprise, given Palace's recent image, that no new players arrived during the summer, and the major change was one of presentation. The claret and blue, which had been a part of Palace's playing strip since the club was founded, was replaced by scarlet and royal blue stripes, a change anticipated by the cover of the previous season's programme, where a primary red stood for claret, which was more difficult to print. In order to comply with a progressive image, the nickname was changed inexplicably from The Glaziers to The Eagles, and a new crest designed accordingly, which mercifully retained a depiction of the original Crystal Palace building itself. Another gimmick, thankfully a short-lived one, was the printing of bogus nicknames in the programme alongside each player's name, so Tony Taylor became 'The Road Runner', Alan Whittle 'The Hustler', and so on, titles which also embellished their track-suit tops.

ALAN WHITTLE

With Allison in charge, Palace were guaranteed more publicity than any other Second Division club, and the concensus before the season began was that a side containing so many well known names would bounce straight back into Division One. In typical Allison style, after losing the first game 4-1 at home to Notts County, the manager confidently predicted that "we won't just get promotion, we'll win the Second Division championship", and he clearly believed it. Encouraged by the promise shown by Jim Cannon, Allison gave sporadic first team chances to other youth team players

MALCOLM ALLISON

Nicky Chatterton and Dave Swindlehurst, and kept faith in Bill Roffey as cover for the injured Paddy Mulligan. Martin Hinshelwood, who had played 16 games the season before despite a recurring back injury, was joined for a few games by his brother Paul, at that time an aspiring centre forward, but without doubt the most controversial choice was that of Paul Hammond in goal in place of John Jackson. Allison insisted that Hammond deserved his place on merit, but it seems more likely that the manager was determined to break with the old regime regardless, and Jackson was the ultimate symbol of that recent past, although most fans will agree that he kept Palace in Division One far longer than they deserved. After two games during which Hammond was mercilessly barracked by sections of the crowd, Jackson had a run of five games back in goal, but after being blamed for two of Cardiff's goals in a 3-3 draw, he was dropped again, and soon afterwards moved to Orient, an undignified end to his glorious Palace career. By this time, Orient were managed by former Palace trainer George Petchey, coached by Terry Long, and now had five ex-Palace players in the side, Jackson and Roffey joining David Payne, Gerry Queen and Phil Hoadley. Ironically, Orient went desperately close to winning promotion themselves at the end of the season, while Palace went rapidly downhill.

Following that Cardiff game, and with his team badly adrift at the bottom of the Second Division, Allison made his first two signings – Derek Jeffries and Roy Barry – and threw them together in central defence, dropping both Mel Blyth and Iain Philip. Jeffries had been one of Allison's proteges at Maine Road, and as a 15 year-old he had described him as "one of the best prospects since Bobby Moore". Certainly he looked a cut above the usual centre half in terms of skill, but his new partner was a classic example of a 'stopper'. Roy

DEREK JEFFRIES

Barry, a Scot, was a hard man who had recovered from a badly broken leg and regained his place at Coventry only to lose it, strangely enough, to John Craven, whom Allison had rejected as a forward. Barry's arrival left no place for Bobby Bell, and after failing to attract any interest on the transfer market he went to try his luck in South Africa.

The new-look defence, with Mulligan having apparently recovered from his knee injury, didn't really improve matters, though, and with Whittle and Possee having failed to score a single goal between them, Allison's next move was for Southend winger Peter Taylor, which signalled the start of a steady improvement. Until now, Palace had been playing without true wingers, since Don Rogers had dropped back to a deeper position, in keeping with Allison's philosophy, the cornerstone of which was a belief in the short pass. Taylor's great strength was his crossing ability, and although he didn't score too many goals in his first season, he had a hand in the majority of Palace's goals, and gave the fans something to get excited about once again. Until now, Possee and Whittle had received most balls with their backs to the goal, and were failing to make clear chances for themselves, but now Peter Taylor was getting behind defences and lashing in the kind of crosses which neither Don Rogers or Charlie Cooke had been capable of. Unfortunately, Possee and Whittle were two of the shortest forwards in the league, and were hardly a menace to defenders in the air, so Allison signed Mick Hill, a centre forward from Ipswich, who did a lot of the donkey work up front without managing to score. With two new forwards in the side, Cooke and Tambling were released, and Palace made their final signings for the season, Jeff Johnson and Stewart Jump.

On Boxing Day of 1973, Palace suffered the humiliation of losing 3-0 to the exiles at Orient, and went into the new year still in bottom place, with Malcolm Allison doggedly defending his conviction that Palace would turn the corner, and refusing to resign. The first day of 1974 saw Palace line up against West Bromwich Albion with only two survivors from the season's first game, Paul Hammond and Don Rogers, and the 1-0 victory began an astonishing run of thirteen games with just two defeats, which miraculously lifted them at one stage to fourth from bottom, one place clear of relegation. Derek Possee returned from injury to score eight goals in ten games, and despite a vote of confidence from the board, Malcolm Allison not only survived, but seemed vindicated. However, the recovery proved to have come too late after such a

JEFF JOHNSON

diabolical start, and Palace were finally relegated for the second year running, despite playing some genuinely good football and attracting large crowds. The tragedy was that if Allison had compromised his ideals even slightly, then they might have avoided the drop, but pragmatism wasn't in his make-up, and that has been his downfall ever since.

1974-75

Despite relegation, Malcolm Allison had at last got his players performing approximately according to his theories, and there was no doubt in anybody's mind that Palace's stay in the Third Division would be brief, given the improved quality of football seen in the latter half of the season. Although the team began this new campaign with very little difference in personnel – only Derek Possee had gone inevitably to Brisbane Road – some very significant changes were imminent, which were to have a lasting effect on the club.

A couple of good early results were a 6-2 defeat of Swindon and an impressive 5-1 victory over Watford in the League Cup, which was Palace's best game to date under Allison. It seemed that confidence in a quick return to Division Two was reasonable, but the manager surprised everyone by releasing two players who one would have thought were crucial to

MEL BLYTH

the side. Mel Blyth, who had re-established himself in central defence, and who was the final link with Bert Head's promotion winners of 1969, was sold to Southampton, and Don Rogers, easily Palace's top scorer in each of his two seasons, moved up two divisions to join Queens Park Rangers. The two players who moved in the opposite direction from Loftus Road were Terry Venables, a famous player well past his prime, and a young Welsh

centre back, Ian Evans. Malcolm Allison, justifying his decision to release Blyth, succeeded in damning him with faint praise, but was certainly accurate in the comparison with his replacement: "Mel is a very competent all round defender but I felt we needed more power in the air and in this respect Ian Evans is brilliant." Regarding Don Rogers, the implication was that the much younger Peter Taylor, already being noticed by the England manager Don Revie, had overshadowed Rogers since his arrival, and the opportunity to sign Venables – a good friend of Allison's – would be of more benefit to the club. In fact, Allison already had Venables earmarked as a potential coach, but his sixteen appearances as a player helped to consolidate Palace's position amongst the Third Division leaders. Venables' playing style had always been in accordance with Allison's ideals, relying on accurate passing and conservation of energy, but his physical limitations made things very difficult for him in the rough and tumble of the lower divisions and he wisely decided to finish his playing days at the surprisingly young age of 31, and concentrate on his burgeoning career in management. Indeed, shortly after leaving QPR for Palace, there was speculation that he might return to replace the Rangers manager Gordon Jago, but Venables quickly pledged his future to Selhurst Park, happy for the moment to work as Malcolm Allison's assistant. The signing of the 22 year-old Ian Evans turned out to be Allison's best transfer manoeuvre for Palace, and he immediately became the first choice in the middle of the defence, teaming up with Derek Jeffries once Roy Barry had lost his place after a sudden attack of pleurisy.

Undoubtedly the inspiration for the side was Peter Taylor, who scored for the England Under-21's on his debut, and went on to play for the senior side while still in the Third Division with Palace, but another player who made an important contribution was Mark Lindsay, one of several youth players thrown into the first team by Allison. Lindsay was used mainly in a defensive midfield position, and occasionally as a genuine sweeper, and was central to Palace's success in the first part of the season. He was quick to the loose ball and accurate in his passing, and exemplified the policy at that time of building attacks from deep positions. Sadly, he lost his form after a good start and was superseded at first by Nicky Chatterton, the groundsman's son, and then by Martin Hinshelwood, both of whom were colleagues of Lindsay in the youth team, and both prone to repeated injuries. At one stage of the season, with Jim Cannon and Dave Swindlehurst established in the side, the average age of the outfield players was under 21, a reflection of the manager's abiding belief in youth. Swindlehurst, who had started only four first team games the year before, eventually emerged as the best option at centre forward, seeing off Mick Hill and the briefly on-loan Wyn Davies, and went on to finish

America. It wasn't long, though, before Peter Wall was back in the reckoning, this time after a bout of hepatitis, and Mulligan's patchy Palace career ended with him moving on to West Bromwich Albion.

PADDY MULLIGAN

Despite an excellent start to the season, which saw Palace on top of the division at the beginning of October after four straight wins, results began to dip as Winter approached, and a sequence of seven games with only one victory pushed them down to sixth place, although still well in touch. Malcolm Allison was clear about the reason for this decline, blaming the poor state of the pitches for reducing matches to lotteries, and advocating a Winter break in the season. He showed his true colours with the splendid cry of "How can you expect an artist to work in these conditions?", in spite of which his next purchase was the artisan Phil Holder from Spurs. Holder's efforts, tireless though they were, could not help to raise Palace into a promotion place, and they eventually finished in a disappointing fifth position, although only a few points away from third place. In the end, it was the form away from home against eminently beatable sides that let them down, together with too many drawn games at home, and once again a lot of entertaining football had led nowhere. Yet despite this, the crowd

LEN CHATTERTON

joint top scorer with 15 goals. He had apparently conquered his terrible pre-match nerves thanks to Allison's novel psychological approach, and another player to benefit from this emphasis on a positive mental attitude was Paddy Mulligan, who won his place back from Stewart Jump after being inspired by a series of films on sports psychology from

had stayed loyal, at between 15 and 20 thousand, which was exceptional for the Third Division, and Allison's flair for publicity undoubtedly endeared him to the fans, regardless of his conspicuous lack of success.

PHIL HOLDER

In the final game of the season, with their promotion chance gone, Palace lost in front of a miserable crowd of 2,025 at Tranmere, who were already relegated to the Fourth Division. Not a game worthy of too much interest, perhaps, except that it saw the debut of another youngster, the 16-year-old left back Kenny Sansom, who was to develop into one of the outstanding players of all time for both Crystal Palace and England.

1975-76

Once again Palace were among the favourites for promotion, and this time it looked a certainty for most of the season, after five straight wins had given them their best start ever. The foundation of their success was an excellent defence, comprised of the rejuvenated Peter Wall, now playing at right back, Jim Cannon at left back, Ian Evans with Derek Jeffries in the centre and goalkeeper Paul Hammond back in the team after losing his place temporarily to Tony Burns. Peter Taylor, Nicky Chatterton, Martin Hinshelwood and Phil Holder made up the midfield, while up front Dave Swindlehurst had a new partner in David Kemp. Kemp had been signed from non-league Slough Town, leaving the transfer-listed Alan Whittle scrapping unhappily in the reserves, and he made a good start for Palace, scoring seven goals in the first eight games, but it was Ian Evans who earned the headlines with a wonderful hat-trick against Colchester. This was quite a feat for any Palace player, let

TONY BURNS

alone a defender, and it was the first since Barry Dyson's in 1966. Indeed, since Evans, the trick has only been repeated by out and out centre forwards – Swindlehurst, Allen, Flanagan, Wright and Bright – and this illustrates the value of his contribution to attack as well as to a sound defence. Like most footballers, Evans obeyed a catalogue of

superstitions, a particularly revolting one being the habit of always chewing the same bit of gum throughout the game, which involved sticking it on the bench at half-time and popping it back in his mouth for the second half. One of the less obscure footballer's superstitions is the habit of not having a hair cut during a cup run, a tradition which died out during the spikey-topped 1980s, but which was widespread in the shaggy '70s. This meant some pretty dishevelled hairstyles in the Palace team this season, because this was the year of the great cup run, the abiding symbol of which was 'Mal's Fedora'.

By the time of the first round of the F.A.Cup, Palace were already clear at the top of the Third Division, having only lost once in 18 games, and must have fancied their chances at home to Isthmian League side Walton & Hersham. Victory was achieved only narrowly, with David Kemp scoring from close range against several of his former Slough team mates, and on that evidence few people would have imagined that Palace would progress to the semi-finals. That they did so well owed something to the fact that they were drawn away from home in every round from then on, since Palace's away form in the league that season was spectacular, and they actually ended the season with more points earned on their travels than at home. With Palace now a feared team, sides would come to Selhurst Park determined to go away with a point, but on their own grounds they found they could not match Palace when it came to an open game of football. Having beaten Millwall after a replay in the second round, the third round of the cup saw the 2-1 defeat of another non-league side, Scarborough, but not too many people would have shared Malcolm Allison's optimism when the draw for the fourth round paired his team with First Division Leeds United, at Elland Road. David Swindlehurst's headed goal from Taylor's free kick completed a genuine piece of giant-killing, and this victory gave the team fresh confidence after a surprising loss of form in the league during December, although Palace had built up such an impressive lead that despite four consecutive defeats they still entered the new year on top of Division Three.

Allison's hunger for publicity was never more evident, and he was constantly pictured in a variety of poses, from brandishing his big cigar and daft hat to sharing a bath with Fiona Richmond, then notorious as a purveyor of soft porn. The fans had been used to media exposure since Allison's arrival but now, with the players having made a record, and cheap replicas of the fedora on sale, all sorts of people were professing themselves lifelong supporters, and a whole generation of Croydon schoolboys were suddenly proudly sporting red and blue scarves. Victory in the fifth round was somehow inevitable, and it came against Chelsea at Stamford Bridge. Palace took a 2-0

NICKY CHATTERTON

lead through Taylor and Chatterton before Chelsea drew level, only for Taylor to score an unforgettable winner direct from a free kick. By now, Alan Whittle had fought his way back into the side, and it was his last ever goal for Palace that won the sixth round tie against the leading Second Division side Sunderland, and put them into the semi-final for the first time in their history. The players had got there by quite simply playing a quality of football that their more illustrious opponents

– Leeds, Chelsea and Sunderland – couldn't hope to match, and allied to excellent tactical organisation was the total belief in themselves that made Palace special, which is why Malcolm Allison will always command affection from the fans who were around then.

MARTIN HINSHELWOOD

Despite these famous victories Palace had now slipped down the league table to third place after too many mediocre home performances, and they also suffered the loss of Martin Hinshelwood for the rest of the season, hospitalised for a cartilege operation. Hinshelwood was never truly fit ever again, and although he played a handful of games over the next two seasons, he was eventually forced to retire from the game at the age of 24. It is quite difficult to assess his influence on the team, because although he was by no means spectacular, he was a dedicated disciple of Allison and Venables, and was arguably the most intelligent member of Palace's midfield.

As Palace prepared for their semi-final, against Southampton at Stamford Bridge, Malcolm Allison made another of his confident predictions; "Palace and Derby. That's my forecast for the Cup Final on May 1st.", and he went on to tempt fate by looking forward to appearing in next season's European Cup-

Winners Cup. Although Southampton were pressing for promotion from the Second Division, many people made Palace favourites to reach the final, comparing their cup run with that of the Saints, who had taken the easier route of overcoming Aston Villa, Blackpool, West Brom and Bradford. Far from being over confident, on the day the Palace players were paralysed by nerves, and they performed nowhere near their best. After Peter Taylor had gone off injured early on, there was no source of inspiration, and Southampton won rather comfortably, by two goals to nil, surprised at the absence of any threat to their own goalmouth.

The feeling of anti-climax was certainly felt very strongly by the fans at the game, who had come to believe in Allison's prophecies, and the same sense of disappointment spread throughout the players, who completely lost any sense of purpose in the remaining league games. They won only one out of seven, and amazingly missed out on promotion once again, having looked the biggest certainties ever earlier in the season. Needing to win the final two games to go up, Palace could only draw 0-0 at home to a mediocre Chesterfield, and it was hard for the fans to swallow the fact that the season had so quickly turned so sour. If Palace had reached the Cup Final, then Malcolm Allison's extravagent boasts would have been acceptable, but I suspect that a quieter approach, of the kind favoured by Steve Coppell in 1990, might have seen them at least concentrate harder on their league position, and gain something from an extraordinary season. As it was, Allison's three years ended with him leaving 'by mutual consent' and being succeeded naturally by his deputy, Terry Venables. Although known as a showman himself, Venables had until now appeared thoughtful and dignified in comparison to Big Mal, and he was now ready for his next step towards his ultimate goal, the job of England manager.

1976-77

In many ways, Allison's most tangible achievement at the club was the development of a strong youth policy, which began to bear fruit just as he left, enabling Terry Venables to enjoy the benefit and much of the credit. The first of the crop to make the first team was Kenny Sansom, who had looked outstanding in the few games he had played after Palace's semi-final defeat, and Venables immediately installed him as first choice left back. Cannon moved into the centre alongside Evans, precipitating the departure of Derek Jeffries back up North to Chester, and Peter Wall made up a back four that was the best the club has had.

Venables declared his intentions for the future by predicting early on some others of the youth team players likely to break into the first team during the season, naming Neil Smillie, Vince Hilaire, Ian Walsh and Peter Caswell. In addition, Paul Hinshelwood, who had already been converted from a centre forward to a full back in the reserves, was being groomed to take over from Peter Wall. As it was, he came into the side sooner than expected, but as a midfield replacement for his brother Martin.

Yet another change of playing strip saw the adoption of another supposedly continental style, the diagonal red and blue sash across a white shirt replacing the previous design, which was apparently "too drab and dark, especially under floodlights". I don't remember anyone complaining about it, and I suspect that the change had more to with the new manager's commercial instincts.

Venables' obsession with continental football also manifested itself in an exaggerated version of Allison's passing game, which frustrated the fans, with each move being built slowly and deliberately from the back, and possession being paramount. In a way, the departure of the more flamboyant Peter Taylor to Spurs can be seen as a necessary part of the Venables

plan, and although the fans were sad to see him go, he was obviously too talented to stay in the Third Division, having already won four England caps, and he went with their blessing.

Alan Whittle had left for Orient and David Kemp was soon to move on to Portsmouth, but Venables had already signed a couple of unknown players as potential replacements – the not very loveable rogues, Barry Silkman and Rachid Harkouk. Harkouk was a wayward attacker with an occasionally explosive shot, which earned him the inevitable nickname of 'Rash the Smash', while Silkman was an out

BARRY SILKMAN

and out winger who had fallen out with his last manager at Hereford. John Sillett had wanted him to work on running back, covering and tackling rather than concentrating on attack, principles that characterise that manager to this day at tedious cost to followers of Coventry City.

In contrast to the wonderful start to the 1975-76 season, early results were rather disappointing and for most of the season it looked as though Palace would end up missing out on promotion once again, although this time the results at home were excellent. In an extremely closely matched division, though, there were rarely less than ten sides within a few points of a promotion place, and Palace were always threatening to put together a string of results, it being widely acknowledged that they were potentially a cut above the rest.

In the F.A.Cup, the first round went to two replays against Brighton, the eventual victory coming by a single goal at the neutral ground of Stamford Bridge, and after a comfortable 4-0 result over non-league Enfield, Palace had to travel to face Liverpool in the third round. This time there were no brash predictions of an upset, but Palace organised themselves well and were considered unfortunate to come away only with a goalless draw, largely thanks to a series of good saves by Ray Clemence. Despite Palace leading 1-0 in the replay, Liverpool eventually went through 3-2, and the fans' chorus of "we can concentrate on the league now" was for once a wise thought. By now Venables had added the experienced George Graham to the midfield, enabling Paul Hinshelwood to finally take up his duties at right back, and the reserve team forward Steve Perrin had come in to partner Swindlehurst up front. An experiment with the Indian born

RICKY HEPPOLETTE

Ricky Heppolette proved a flop, though, which meant that Holder and Chatterton kept their places in a reliable, if rather dull midfield. Graham's ability to control the game at his own painfully slow pace served Palace well,

and it was his influence which helped to improve their position at the start of new year into fifth place.

STEVE PERRIN

Scoring goals was proving to be somewhat of a problem, with Perrin being too similar to Swindlehurst in his rather lumbering style, and it was the purchase of Jeff Bourne from Derby County which in the end proved to be the season's turning point. The fee for Bourne came from the sale of goalkeeper Paul Hammond to Tampa Bay Rowdies in the North American Soccer League, where he joined Mark Lindsay, and the fact that Venables felt compelled to justify the £30,000 outlay illustrates that the days of the big money signings were way past, and that Ray Bloye was not prepared to invest in the team, despite having enjoyed bigger crowds than most in the Third Division.

Bourne came to Palace rather overweight from being out of the team at Derby, but once he was fit he made a crucial contribution to the promotion effort, scoring nine goals in his fifteen games, and complementing Swindlehurst nicely. He inspired Palace's best two victories of the season, 5-0 against Swindon and 4-0 against Sheffield Wednesday, and suddenly promotion became a possibility, if still a slim one.

Venables was livid when a rearranged game at Port Vale was played on a waterlogged pitch, after the earlier fixture had been postponed at very short notice due to illness and injury among the opposition. Vale won 4-1 with George Graham sent off in a bad tempered game, and once again Palace were written off for the season with four games remaining and six points to make up on third placed Wrexham. However, two of the four games were against the Welsh side themselves, and after winning at Chesterfield, and at home to Wrexham and Lincoln City, Palace's final game of the season saw them travelling to the Racecourse Ground in midweek needing to win by two clear goals to even have a chance of going up. Since Wrexham had not lost at home all season, the odds looked very much against Palace.

The manner of Palace's victory that evening is still hard to believe. After Swindlehurst and Perrin had made it 2-0 to Palace, Wrexham

RACHID HARKOUK

woke up and fought back to 2-2, which remained the scoreline until the last minute of the game. When Harkouk scored Palace's third on the stroke of full time, it still didn't seem to matter much to the celebrating Welsh supporters, but straight from the restart, and in injury time, Jeff Bourne – fittingly – made the score 4-2 and completed an unforgettable night.

I only wish I could claim I was there, but the elation I felt when hearing the score on the radio must have been magnified in the hearts of those at the game, and many were moved to tears at the remarkable manner of the victory, and at the prospect of promotion from the Third Division, although this was still not certain. Wrexham were completely shattered by the result, and although they could still have gone up at Palace's expense, they lost their final game against the champions Mansfield, and Terry Venables won promotion to Division Two in his first season as a manager, one of the few minor honours he has so far achieved in English football.

Of the three promoted teams, it was the champions, Mansfield, who fared worst in the Second Division, ultimately being relegated after just one season. Palace and Brighton, always very closely matched, both looked at home straight away, and in the end it was the Seagulls, a team which Alan Mullery had built around Mark Lawrenson and the talented Peter Ward, who narrowly missed promotion to the First Division. It is of note that from 1974 to 1981, over a period of seven seasons, Palace and Brighton were always in the same division as each other, winning promotion at the same time as they progressed from the Third to the First. The rivalry that has built up between the two sets of supporters was fuelled when Venables and Mullery had a public slanging match after a particularly bad tempered game, the Brighton manager calling Palace a team of "animals", and Mullery has been despised ever since at Selhurst Park, not least for his vulgar gestures to the Palace fans.

TERRY VENABLES

It was Palace who started the season best, winning their first two games against Millwall and Mansfield, and moving into third place with seven games played. Venables gave further indication of his faith in the players who had won the F.A.Youth Cup by introducing two more of them into the team

alongside Sansom, namely Peter Nicholas and Vince Hilaire. Nicholas was at this stage perceived as a defender and only played a couple of early games as cover for injured players, but Hilaire was given a good run as an inside forward rather than the more orthodox winger he was to become. A surprise inclusion for the team against Mansfield was Martin

PETER NICHOLAS

Hinshelwood, who had supposedly retired the year before, but who had been kept on the staff to help with coaching. With George Graham and Phil Holder both injured, Venables was forced to press Hinshelwood into the midfield and he played well, even scoring a goal, before being substituted late in the game.

Having beaten Brentford over two legs in the first round of the League Cup, Palace were given a chance for revenge over the F.A.Cup winners Southampton in the second round, but threw it away by missing a penalty in a goalless draw during which the referee sent off Phil Boyer for head-butting Jim Cannon, and Cannon for retaliating. In the replay at The Dell, which went to extra time, Southampton were leading 2-1 when Palace were awarded a penalty on the stroke of full time. Jeff Bourne's spot kick was saved but George Graham followed up to put the ball in the net for the equaliser. As the players left the field, most of them shared the belief of the crowd that 2-2 was the final score, but it transpired that the referee had disallowed the goal, ruling that full time was up the moment the goalkeeper had saved the original shot. Never one to take defeat graciously, Terry Venables had a good old moan about being cheated by the referee, although he had in fact made the correct decision.

Putting this setback behind them, Palace went on to beat Sheffield United and leaders Bolton in the league, despite George Graham being sent off again, to stay in touch at the top. The programme for the next game, against Fulham, included an item about Ian Evans, who had by

GEORGE GRAHAM

now played 13 times for Wales and was looking forward to the imminent World Cup qualifier against Scotland, for which he was an automatic choice. The Fulham game changed the whole direction of Palace's season, and brought Evans' career for both Palace and Wales to a cruel end. The once great George Best was now playing for Fulham, and when he and Evans went for a loose ball around the halfway line they arrived at exactly the same time; the cracking of bone produced an unmistakeable sound that could be heard by all 28,343 people in the crowd. Best was unscathed, but Ian Evans had sustained a double fracture to his right leg which put him

in hospital for months.

The loss of Evans affected Palace's form very badly, and their position deteriorated steadily to that of a mid-table side, which on reflection turned out to be a blessing for Venables, giving him a very convenient opportunity to experiment with his young players. He was constantly being asked why he didn't buy anyone to strengthen the team and push for promotion, and he was always clear with his reply; Bloye wouldn't give him any money. He believed, however, that the youth team, now heading towards a second successive F.A.Youth Cup victory, would form the basis of his side for next season, and with the breathing space created by having earned points early on, he devoted the rest of the year to his experiments.

The first task, though, was to replace Evans at centre back, because the optimistic forecasts of an early recovery were soon found to be far from true. Peter Wall played there for a few games, and then Mel Blyth came back from Southampton on a three month loan, forming a nostalgic link with the days of Bert Head, which now seemed light years away. Next into the number six shirt was Peter Nicholas, soon to be succeeded by Billy Gilbert, who formed a partnership with Jim Cannon that was to last for the next six years.

Venables knew that the current team would not last too long in the First Division if they were elevated too soon, so he was ruthless in his purge of anyone who wasn't either young enough or good enough to have a part to play for the next few years, and started to trim his squad in preparation for next season. The first to go was Jeff Bourne, who signed for Dallas Tornado, followed by Peter Wall and Stewart Jump. Steve Perrin was then sold to Plymouth for £35,000, and Neil Smillie and Tony Burns went to America on loan for the rest of the season. To replace Burns, Venables invested £40,000 in Aston Villa's John Burridge, the classic goalkeeping clown and Bruce Grobbelaar's role model, who instantly became popular with the fans after years of enduring the grim countenances of Burns and Hammond.

players were already representing their countries at youth level, and were showing great promise for the future, and everything seemed on the up and up. The great surprise, given this anticipation of imminent success, was that it actually happened.

BILLY GILBERT

Palace's final position of ninth in Division Two was a good one considering the experimental nature of the team and their extreme youth, especially when one realises that five of the players – Nicholas, Gilbert, Hilaire, Murphy and Fenwick – were combining their first team duties with playing in the Youth Cup. Venables had done well to completely transform the team bequeathed to him by Malcolm Allison, without having been able to spend much money, and after two years only Chatterton, Cannon, Swindlehurst and Sansom remained.

The celebrity status of Terry Venables was being enhanced with a T.V. serialisation of his 'Hazell' books, co-written with Gordon Williams, and at the same time as he was coining it in from that, the board of directors were busy concocting a deal with Sainsburys, which the present chairman Ron Noades has implied lined their own pockets at the club's severe long term expense. Several of the young

1978-79

It is worth taking a close look at the team that won promotion at the end of this season in some detail, because as well as being the best ever seen at Palace, it was certainly the most settled, with the smallest number of players to be used in the course of the season – only 18, including Barry Silkman's one appearance as a substitute. The oldest player in the squad at the start of the season was goalkeeper John Burridge, at 26. As well as being a dedicated

JOHN BURRIDGE

crowd pleaser – he would endeavour to make the most straightforward save look spectacular – he kept the defence going throughout the game with constant shouted instructions, and his enthusiasm for the game was contagious. Right back Paul Hinshelwood was a much better player in that position than as a striker, and was still only 22, while Sansom at left back was so exceptionally gifted that he was already in the reckoning for a place in the England team at the age of 19. In central defence Jim Cannon, already in his seventh season in the first team, was not yet 25, but was a seasoned old pro. compared to his 18-year-old partner Billy Gilbert, whose physical toughness belied his youth. Three more 18-year-olds, Murphy, Nicholas and Hilaire combined with 24-year-old Nicky Chatterton in midfield, and the top scorer for the past three seasons, Dave Swindlehurst, was still

only 21.

With Harkouk having gone to Q.P.R. and Silkman shortly to join Malcolm Allison at Plymouth, the attack was augmented by the £180,000 signing of Mike Elwiss from Preston, who kept Ian Walsh out of the side for the first dozen games. Elwiss was the latest and most promising in a growing list of partners up front for Swindlehurst, succeeding Mick Hill, Dave Kemp, Steve Perrin and Jeff Bourne. He had once been on the verge of signing for Liverpool four years earlier while at Doncaster, but the deal fell through when the club bumped up his price at the last minute. Although not a very prolific goalscorer to start with, Elwiss was a skilful ball player of the type Venables has always admired, and his influence resulted in Palace's neat passing moves being extended into the penalty area, with speculative long range shots becoming a rarity.

Although most people expected Palace to be among the front runners once again, even the fans were surprised at how well the season began, with them quickly going to the top of the table and remaining unbeaten for 11 games. Evidence that this was to be Palace's lucky season came in the 1-1 home draw with West Ham, with Billy Gilbert's fluked goal from his own half reminiscent of John Sewell's famous punt against Leeds years earlier.

In the League Cup it took First Division Aston Villa two replays to get past Palace, with the final 3-0 scoreline at Coventry's neutral ground being easily the heaviest defeat of the season, and the only time all year that John Burridge let in more than two goals. Indeed, it is unlikely that Palace's defensive record for the season – 24 goals conceded in 42 league games – will ever be equalled, and has certainly never been approached since. To attribute Palace's success simply to the defence, though, would be a mistake, because the essence of their game was controlled posession in every area of the field – Venables' European dream realised in the English Second Division. In midfield the cocksure Jerry Murphy was already a master of first time control and accurate passing, and Peter Nicholas, although less adventurous with the ball, invariably found himself in the right position to either attack or defend. The genuine element of flair came from Vince Hilaire, outrageously skilful although inconsistent, and always looking for the chance to get the ball at his feet and go past the full back. The final component which made the midfield complete was the signing of Steve Kember from Leicester, which meant Chatterton finally moving on to Millwall. Kember's return to Selhurst Park after seven years away turned out to be an inspired move, but in fact Venables only intended to buy him and defender Tony Hazell as squad members, to cover for likely

PAUL HINSHELWOOD

injuries to the younger players. Kember's experience and undiluted passion for the game was exactly what the other players needed to sustain their impetus to the end of the season, and with George Graham unable to regain his first team place, Kember was able to help Palace into the First Division for the second time in his career. The surprising thing was the lack of injuries throughout the season, and despite Hinshelwood being out for two months after a cartilege operation, with Terry Fenwick substituting at right back, the major problem

was a similar injury to Mike Elwiss half way through the season, from which he never fully recovered.

Having started the season so well, a slight dip in results after Christmas, with seven draws from nine games, served as a warning against complacency, and a promising F.A.Cup run was thwarted in the fifth round with a surprising home defeat at the hands of Wolves. Come the spring, however, the young players blossomed again, with Ian Walsh proving an admirable replacement for Elwiss up front, and the defence becoming even meaner, conceding only five goals in the final 17 games. Remarkably, with only three games to go, Palace were occupying their lowest position of the whole season – fourth behind Stoke, Brighton and Sunderland – and with no apparently easy fixtures remaining. Venables had been saying all season that with no outstanding team in the Division nothing would be decided until the final kick, and so it proved.

The 2-0 home victory over a very ordinary Notts County was comprehensive enough, but it was the next game, at Orient's cramped Brisbane Road ground, that was to prove crucial, for a defeat would in the event have condemned Palace to another frustrating year in Division Two. The latter half of the season had taught the players to fight for possession when they weren't being given space by the opposition and this quality, typified by Steve Kember more than anyone, enabled them to scrape through a tense game and hang on to the narrow lead provided by Swindlehurst's goal.

That victory, under such pressure against a good side, boosted their confidence and that of the fans, so that when it came to the last game – a rearranged fixture against Burnley on the friday night before the Cup Final – an amazing crowd of 51,482 turned out to witness another piece of Selhurst Park history, a crowd figure that will never be equalled. Promotion was still not certain, with at least a point needed to climb above Sunderland in third place, but in the event the passionate atmosphere, enhanced as always under the floodlights, inspired Palace to play as well as they had all year. This was a bit of a surprise, given that the imperative was simply not to lose, which can very often result in bad games.

youngsters, and he deserved a great deal of credit for constructing a team in his own image, playing in a style that was unique among the lower divisions.

IAN WALSH

Ian Walsh's precisely aimed header put Palace ahead and when Swindlehurst made it 2-0 from close range we all knew that we were worthy champions ahead of Brighton and Stoke. The players and the ecstatic fans celebrated promotion together and I set off on my moped, replaying the goals in my head and feeling dangerously delirious. Time had shrunk, and the ten year old boy innocently cheering Mark Lazarus on his lap of honour against Fulham in 1969 had become a twenty year old celebrating the same feeling of pure joy.

Palace had made it to Division One by sticking uncompromisingly to the principles introduced by Malcolm Allison five years earlier, although his teams had never quite been able to put them into practice. Whereas some of Allison's players would not be convinced of the value of patience and cautious possession, Venables was able to start from scratch with his

1979-80

At long last, having made it to the First Division on a shoestring, Ray Bloye granted his manager some money to spend, and Venables could hardly contain his relief at being able to buy two 'big name' players. Gerry Francis, erstwhile England captain, had always been prone to injury but was still regarded as one of the country's most sophisticated midfield players, while Mike Flanagan – a prolific scorer for Charlton – was also renowned for a punch-up on the pitch with his bearded partner Derek Hales. It is difficult to imagine now, but at this time Flanagan was being touted as a possibility for the England team. In fact his style was very similar to that of the luckless Mike Elwiss, but without that player's cutting edge, and he eventually found his best position later in his

MIKE FLANAGAN

career in QPR's midfield. Flanagan, then, started the season in place of Ian Walsh up front, and Francis took over from Kember, who Venables did not consider up to playing in Division One, having served his purpose.

These two additions to the side did nothing to disrupt the cohesion of the team, and the quality of football played in the first couple of months of the season quickly dispelled the doubts that many people had about the true worth of Venables' young stars. Vince Hilaire, in particular, was looking exceptional and thriving on the service from an occasionally

brilliant Francis. Jerry Murphy, reaching his peak tragically early in his career, epitomised the energy-saving approach to midfield play so favoured by Venables. Kenny Sansom, having played his first game for England in the post-season home international game against Wales, was already acknowledged as peerless in that position, and even Jim Cannon was looking like a player of International class.

Early results tended to suggest a difficult time ahead, with draws against Manchester City, Southampton and Middlesborough followed by another stalemate in the League Cup against Stockport, twice Palace's conquerers in that competition during the 1970s. Suddenly though, everything clicked and within a week they had beaten Derby County 4-0, and then slaughtered Stockport 7-0 in the home leg of the cup tie, with Flanagan scoring twice in each game. These two results set up a run of games during which Palace beat Aston Villa, Stoke and finally Ipswich, to end September at the top of Division One, along the way earning Terry Venables a bottle of whiskey. The victory over Ipswich, still one of the division's better teams, was the apogee of what Palace had been working towards since Allison's time; every player was constantly thinking about his position in relation to the play, and each seemed able to find space and time to control the ball and pass accurately to a team mate. The principle seems very simple , but only Liverpool have been able to perfect it consistently in England, making it virtually impossible for lesser players to compete on equal terms. And although it might be heretical to say so, at times it becomes very boring. When the system works, however, good results will keep the fans happy, and Palace's result against Ipswich was executed with such efficiency that the score might well have been extended. Particularly enjoyable was the fourth goal, started and finished by a rampant Jim Cannon, having the time of his life; he won the ball in his own half, laid it out to the left, and timed his run into the box perfectly to meet the cross with a sweet volley.

JIM CANNON

In moving to the top of the table with such style, the amount of publicity in the media reached a new level, beyond even Malcolm Allison's wildest dreams, and whichever hack coined the phrase "The Team of the Eighties" provided his fellows with an easy reference point for whatever they wrote about Palace for the next decade – most of it snide. At the time, though, the comment was all favourable, and it was easy to believe that Venables was in charge of a team capable of challenging the likes of Liverpool and Nottingham Forest at their own game. Dreams of the championship, and at the very least qualifying for Europe, were commonplace, and I have yet to hear a satisfactory theory for why everything went quite so badly wrong. The usual explanation is that the players were too green to handle the considerable pressure of success and lavish praise; whilst that is undoubtedly true of Sansom, it does not explain why the combined wisdom of Terry Venables and his lieutenant Gerry Francis could not keep them on a straight course towards the success of which they were surely capable. One thing is certain, that there was only one way to go, and Palace went that way with a vengeance for the next five years, with little respite and precious little to cheer.

Directly after reaching the heights by beating Ipswich, Palace stumbled to a run of five games without a win, and although still playing well enough, the extravagent claims of greatness became tempered. The 'Team of the Eighties' tag was still in vogue, though, and two excellent victories followed; against Manchester City, now managed by Malcolm Allison, and – for the only time to date in the league – against Terry Neill's Arsenal. The City game was the most entertaining of the season, with extensive coverage on T.V., and reaffirmed Palace's reputation as a genuine force in the First Division. Also notable was a 1-0 victory over Brian Clough's Nottingham Forest team, then the reigning European Champions. By now, though, Palace had fallen down to eighth position, and the players were beginning to believe too much in their own publicity. They couldn't understand why the points weren't just falling into their laps,

GERRY FRANCIS

considering how very good they apparently were, and having lost only six of their previous 60 league matches, a run of four defeats from five games came as a new and totally devastating experience to them. Although Venables had taught his players to stay calm and patient when in control of a game, he hadn't equipped them to cope with the crisis of confidence that defeat can bring, and they never again came to resemble the precocious team that had strolled to the top of the league just a couple of months previously.

Already Kenny Sansom was talking about getting away, and his club form at least was in decline, and Jerry Murphy, not for the last

JERRY MURPHY

time, appeared indifferent to what was happening. With goals becoming a rare commodity Dave Swindlehurst was made the scapegoat,and after being dropped in favour of Ian Walsh he was transferred to Derby County. He actually became a more dangerous player after leaving Selhurst Park, but it must be said that at the time he did look rather stale.

After being knocked out of the F.A.Cup at the third attempt by Swansea City, the end of the season became as dull and disappointing as the start had been bright and promising. The best late performance came in the 1-1 draw at Arsenal, where Sansom scored his only goal of the season and Pat Jennings saved a penalty from Gerry Francis, but with only one victory in the last ten games Palace collapsed to finish 13th in the table, still their highest position ever. The backlash had begun, but worse, far worse was to come.

1980-81

During the summer Terry Venables pulled off one of the worst transfer deals ever, with Ken Sansom moving to Arsenal in return for Clive Allen and Paul Barron. The 19-year-old Allen had yet to play for the Gunners since his move from QPR, but was valued at £1 million, and goalkeeper Barron was supposedly worth £400,000. John Burridge was a far better keeper, but was in dispute over pay, and was relegated to the reserves. The new partnership of Flanagan and Allen stimulated the feeble imaginations of the tabloid papers, and the two strikers were more memorable dressing up as the music-hall act for the cameras than they ever were on the pitch, only playing 17 games together in all.

PAUL BARRON

After two early setbacks, being beaten by Liverpool and Spurs, a 5-2 victory over Middlesbrough gave considerable encouragement, with Clive Allen scoring a hat-trick and in the process playing his best ever game in Palace colours. Any fancy ideas were quickly stifled, though, by a sequence of seven league defeats on the trot, Palace's worst run since 1925 and one which was sadly to be repeated later in the season.

By now the relationship between the manager and the board of directors had deteriorated to the point where Venables could no longer see a future for himself at the club, and although he stayed until the end of October he had already lost whatever commitment he may have had. The fans, needless to say, were kept in the dark as to the real reasons for his disenchantment, but one can surmise that Ray Bloye's tightfistedness when it was obvious that the squad needed strengthening had become intolerable after four years with hardly any money being spent; a period during which it must have been absolutely rolling in. Burridge's supposed falling-out with Venables was a red herring, as the two men were shortly reunited at QPR, and in retrospect one could see that Bloye himself was preparing to cut and run, having brought the club to the brink of financial ruin.

When Venables finally resigned, to pursue his plastic fantasy at Loftus Road, readers of the programme for the next home game, against Leicester, were able to read – in his own words – the thoughts of Chairman Bloye; his regret at losing Venables after all he had done for the club. The text of the chairman's message was printed in the space reserved for the manager's regular platitudes, and the words 'Terry Venables' appear, like Banquo's ghost, behind a most unappealing picture of Bloye. The man temporarily in charge of the winning team that day was a long-serving member of the coaching staff – Ernie Walley – but Bloye made it clear that "..we will appoint Terry's successor as soon as possible. We want a young man with a progressive outlook." This certainly appeared to put Walley out of the reckoning, but Jim Cannon led a deputation demanding that the board give him the job, and Ernie Walley was officially appointed to the dubious position of 'Caretaker Manager'.

The new man certainly had the confidence of the players, since he had looked after many of them in their days with the youth team, but despite three wins and a draw from five games – their best spell of a miserable season – they stayed firmly anchored to the foot of the table.

40

The fans foresaw little joy under Walley's management, and were clamouring for the return of Malcolm Allison, recently sacked by Manchester City but still a popular figure with those who had so enjoyed the cup run of 1976.

ERNIE WALLEY

He was the complete opposite of the dour and uncharismatic Walley and their wish came true at the beginning of December when once again Bloye asked Allison to save his bacon. John Burridge, Mike Flanagan and Terry Fenwick bailed out to join Venables at QPR, and were replaced in the team by the second string players Terry Boyle and Tony Sealey. With a badly depleted and demoralised squad, and no chance of spending any money on new players, Allison was left with a hopeless task and Palace managed only a single victory under his brief stewardship. Within a year thay had gone from a team of bright, talented and above all confident players to become disillusioned and completely aimless.

With crowd revenue steadily dropping and relegation looking a certainty, Bloye couldn't get rid of the club quickly enough and didn't have to be asked twice when Ron Noades made him an offer. Like the Tory government blaming their Labour predecessors for all their troubles, Noades quickly set about establishing what a mess he had inherited. One wonders why a shrewd businessman would have bought such a clapped out heap of a club if it really was in such a state, and whether the 'Wimbledon Supremo' Noades was conned. One area of operation which had certainly collapsed was that of youth team development, which had been so beneficial to the club just a few years before but which was now moribund. Quite apart from the state of the finances this was the most damaging legacy of Bloye's reign, and for the next five years the only home grown players to make any impact in the first team were Steve Lovell, Shaun Brooks and Gary Stebbing. It must also be said that to date the situation has hardly improved, with only John Salako and Richard Shaw graduating in the late 1980s, although the successful youth team of 1990 promises to be above average.

DARIO GRADI

Noades wanted to rebuild Crystal Palace in Wimbledon's image, and the first step was to import Dario Gradi as Malcolm Allison's replacement. Sacking Allison was unpopular in any case, but after Gradi had supervised seven straight defeats – and effectively relegation from Division One – he had no chance of winning the crowd's support. Peter Nicholas, about the only player to emerge with any credit from this period, wisely accepted Arsenal's offer to stay in the First Division and in return Palace took on the former local schoolboy star David Price , who had by now become an enthusiastic but ineffective plodder. Making their debuts at the same time were Tommy Langley, off-loaded by Venables from QPR, and Brian Bason. Recently Gradi has proved himself to be a good manager when it comes to developing young players, but as a judge of bargains in the transfer market his record at Palace was less than wonderful.

DAVID PRICE

Palace didn't gain their first win of 1981 until beating Birmingham 3-1 in April, but by then relegation had become a mathematical certainty with five games still to play, and no team can ever have had fewer excuses for going down than Palace had that year. Of the four managers, Venables, Allison and Gradi had enjoyed one win each in charge, with Walley seeing his team victorious on three occasions. The home crowd of 9,820 who witnessed that rare win against Birmingham, and two equally rare goals from Langley, was the worst since 1968, but once again worse was to come, and this time everybody somehow knew it.

1981-82

The name of Tommy Langley has become like some jaded comedian's meaningless catch phrase, a cheap way to get a laugh, but I am prepared to defend him nonetheless. His playing style epitomised Palace's collective approach for the whole season, with endeavour being the only quality in evidence, and with few results. Although he only scored three goals all season no one has tried harder than Langley did for Palace, and for that at least he deserved praise rather than the vilification he received. To say that he was simply useless doesn't tell the whole story, because he was a player who had been extremely good as a youngster at Chelsea and he knew that he

TOMMY LANGLEY

wasn't doing himself justice with his performances at Palace. It must be very frustrating for a striker in particular when he knows that he can do so much better, and since goals are such a clear measure of success or failure it is easy to lose confidence completely. Langley chased everything, but there was little purpose to Palace's play and it was hard to tell what role he was being asked to perform, since he lacked the strength of a classic centre-forward; his partner Walsh was similarly lightweight, and with Clive Allen having returned to QPR to rejoin Venables there was now nobody in the team who knew where the goal was. The deal which took Allen to QPR

involved Steve Wicks – a central defender – moving the other way, and this was another bit of transfer business from which Palace came off badly, after losing the best part of £1 million with the cut-price sale of Flanagan and Francis. With Cannon and Gilbert still a solid partnership in central defence the signing of Wicks seemed a peculiar one at a time when the desperate need was for a striker and a left back, and as things turned out Wicks was injured for most of his short time at Selhurst Park.

Palace at least had the satisfaction of winning a few games early on, which they had forgotten how to do in the woeful season before, but they were dreadfully short of attacking ideas. The midfield of Neil Smillie, David Price, Jerry Murphy and Vince Hilaire was neither robust enough to win the ball or confident enough to use it to any great effect. Gradi's team were given an early opportunity to put one over on Venables' renegades – Burridge, Fenwick, Francis, Flanagan, Allen and Sealy – but on the brand new artificial pitch at Loftus Road an awful game was won not by the best team, but by the least worst. It is incredible to me that it has taken the Football League nearly ten years to decide that the arguments in favour of all-weather surfaces are far outweighed by those against, chief of which is the rotten entertainment value to the spectator.

Complementing the overall naffness of the team during this season was the match-day programme, once again sporting a cartoon cover. One can recognise some of the characters depicted in uncharacteristic action poses – Langley, Barron and Walsh amongst them – and Dario Gradi looking worried as usual, but I always wondered why the long-forgotten Iain Philip stands with his fists clenched in triumph, although I am assured that Jim Cannon is the artist's intended victim.

It was clear before too long that although Gradi was unlikely to repeat Malcolm Allison's feat of immediate relegation to the Third Division, neither was his team going to do any better than finish in a moderate mid-table position. The fans were prepared to be patient, realising as they did that Gradi had hardly any resources at his disposal and the weakest first

KEVIN MABBUTT

team squad for years, but Ron Noades was less forgiving. Following three narrow defeats by Derby, Luton and Blackburn, Gradi was sacked after less than ten months in charge; a period during which he had been forced to sell Peter Nicholas, Gerry Francis, Clive Allen and Tony Sealy, replacing them with David Price, Brian Bason, Billy Hughes and Wicks, who had only played four games. It is unsurprising, then, that most fans felt inclined to blame Noades rather than Gradi for the state of things, and it has taken until today for him to earn any sort of grudging respect. Ironically, Gradi had made his best signing by far just a couple of weeks before his dismissal, when he bought Bristol City's Kevin Mabbutt, brother of the Spurs player Gary and equally likeable. A less shrewd investment was Steve Galliers, who had served under Gradi and Noades at Wimbledon, but who failed to import that team's aggression to Palace's midfield in the few games he played before returning to Plough Lane.

Short of bringing back Malcolm Allison for a

third time, the next most popular choice as manager was Steve Kember, a Palace man through and through who had played in the two promotion sides of 1969 and 1979, and who was now in charge of the youth team. Kember made a good start to the job, with a draw and two wins, but he wasn't able to raise his players above the mediocre, despite the efforts of Mabbutt. If Murphy and Hilaire had been playing at anything like their best then I am sure that Mabbutt would have flourished, but he found himself too often having to drop a long way back to find the ball, and was too rarely in scoring positions. In order to try and put some pace into the forward line, Kember made what looked like a very good signing, that of David Giles from Swansea. Giles had been called 'the Welsh Keegan', simply because of his hairstyle, but he was in fact a fairly straightforward winger, which left the

DAVID GILES

central midfield looking weaker than ever. Murphy had completely lost his way, neither Smillie or Hilaire were ball-winners, Price was injured for most of the rest of the season and Shaun Brooks hadn't really progressed from being a very good England schoolboy. The only time that the midfield began to look more solid was when the return of Wicks allowed Jim Cannon to move forward; this was only a temporary measure though, with

Wicks bizarrely moving back to QPR at a loss as soon as results started to improve. It is ironic that the one position that Kember was never able to fill adequately, apart from centre-forward, was that of an aggressive midfielder in the No.4 shirt, for which he would have been the ideal candidate.

comfortable in the middle of the table, Palace slipped steadily towards the relegation zone, and it wasn't until they beat Wrexham in the penultimate game of the season that safety was assured. After another miserable season many fans wanted Ron Noades to go, but of course it was Steve Kember who got the push, after just six months in the job.

SHAUN BROOKS

The one bright spot of the season was reaching the Sixth round of the F.A.Cup, Palace's best run since the semi-final year of 1976, and the furthest they were to go in the competition for the whole of the 1980s. This time there was no First Division opposition to overcome, and having scraped past Enfield, Bolton and Orient, they faced Venables' hated QPR team for a place in the last four. Such a prize would possibly have saved Kember's managerial skin, but Clive Allen cruelly scored a late winner in a game that should have been Palace's, and it was QPR who progressed, eventually losing to Spurs in the final.

By now Mabbutt was completely alone up front, with Walsh having been sold to Swansea and Langley completely ineffective, but he was looking better and better in a declining team, and seemed to be the only hope for the future – if only Palace would buy another striker to help him out. From being fairly

1982-83

Proof, if any were needed, that Ron Noades was some way out of touch with the feelings of the supporters came when he announced the name of the new manager: Alan Mullery, without doubt the most unpopular choice one could imagine. Mullery had been manager of the Brighton side which finished runners-up

HENRY HUGHTON

in Division Two to Palace in 1979, and then moved on to Charlton, from where Noades headhunted him after a year. This left Palace's South London neighbours to soldier on under the unknown Lennie Lawrence, for which they must be eternally grateful. The bad blood between Palace and Brighton had been at its worst during Mullery's time on the South Coast, and from the moment his appointment was announced the majority of fans – myself included – were convinced that the Chairman had made a dreadful mistake. Noades obviously saw in Mullery the charisma which Gradi and Kember lacked, and an ego to match his own, but he never for a moment threatened to endear himself to Palace fans.

Mullery's first act as manager was to recognise the need for a big striker to replace Langley, but the player he signed was Wrexham's Ian Edwards, the first of a series of forgettable forwards he was to buy over the next two years. He also bought Gary Williams, a left back who had been with him at Brighton, and

with Neil Smillie joining the Seagulls at the same time there was a place in midfield for Kember's last signing, Henry Hughton. As many people predicted, Kevin Mabbutt made a good start by scoring five goals in the first six games, and Palace earned some respectable results at last. But the essential problem remained, with neither Edwards or Langley doing much to help Mabbutt, and the goals soon dried up.

Mullery had declared his intention of buying a new centre-back to allow Cannon to play in midfield but that purchase never materialised, and Cannon's partnership with Billy Gilbert stayed intact for another season. Although Cannon was playing as well as ever, the defence as a whole were looking less and less able to prop up the team, and Hinshelwood and Gilbert had lost their appetite for the game. Gary Williams was soon forced to retire after having a knee operation, and the South African teenager Gavin Nebbeling was drafted into

STEVE LOVELL

the defence, while the young goalkeeper David Fry came into the side in place of Paul Barron, sold to West Bromwich Albion. Steve Lovell was tried in midfield, but lost his place once Jerry Murphy started coming back to his best form, and was sold on to Millwall where he immediately started scoring goals!

Shaun Brooks was unhappy at being left out by Mullery and was put on the transfer list, and all in all it was obvious to the fans that they were paying to watch a very miserable

ALAN MULLERY

bunch of players. By now, though, the number of punters prepared to stump up for that dubious pleasure had dwindled severely; the home gates had fallen within two years from regularly pushing 30,000 to the point where 10,000 was now considered a good crowd, and Ron Noades' pledge to turn the club around within a year was proving as absurd as it had always seemed. Perhaps the most despicable public act by Noades – considering his criticism of the previous regime – was the dismantling of the youth team, who were suddenly withdrawn from their league in the middle of the season. This was justified by Noades as a necessary cost-cutting measure, but as well as being a prematurely cruel blow to several young hopefuls it seemed doubly stupid for a club whose greatest success to date had been built on a strong and active youth policy.

This period of Palace's history was without doubt the most depressing ever, and if it was difficult to understand why any of us kept going to the matches in the early part of the season, it was impossible to comprehend once Kevin Mabbutt was out of the team. The meagre crowd had taken to Mabbutt in a big

way, and it was a genuine tragedy for them and for the team when a bad pelvic injury put him out of the game for a large part of the season, enabling the unimproved Langley back into the side. At about the same time Palace's only other striker – Ian Edwards – fractured a cheekbone; he was quickly replaced by the former Spurs player, Chris Jones, bought from Manchester City, but Jones was even slower and less prolific than Edwards, scoring only three goals in 22 games before moving on to Charlton. The next journeyman to try his luck up front was Ally Brown, the West Bromwich Albion striker who had formed a good partnership at the Hawthorns with Cyril Regis, but who had now lost his place to an exciting young forward called Garry Thompson.

Brown proved to be no more incisive than Langley, Edwards or Jones, and it was only when a half-fit Kevin Mabbutt came back into the team that Palace were able to put together a crucial series of four home wins on the trot to save them from the drop to Division Three; indeed, it wasn't until the very last game of the season – a postponed match against Burnley – that such a fate was avoided. The two teams had met in similar circumstances only four years earlier, in the game which gave Palace the Second Division Championship, but the implications of the result this time around were vastly different. Burnley had already beaten Palace in the League and the F.A.Cup, and had reached the last four of the League Cup by beating Spurs at White Hart Lane. They eventually went out to Liverpool despite winning the second leg of the semi-final, and they had some outstanding young players such as Trevor Steven, Mike Phelan and Brian Laws, but by the end of the season they found themselves in 21st. position and needing to beat Palace to stay up. Every other team had completed their fixtures, and it came down to a straight fight for the third relegation place, with Palace only needing a draw to escape – a dramatic scenario which enticed over 22,000 to Selhurst Park, easily the biggest crowd for two years. For Mullery and Noades the prospect of Third Division football was too awful to contemplate, since there were now very few assetts left to sell off; Barron had gone and Gilbert, Murphy and Hilaire no longer appealed as bright young things. Defeat by Burnley would have had serious long-term consequences for the club, but Ian Edwards returned from injury and with his last touch for Crystal Palace scored the goal that provided ill-deserved salvation for another year.

RON NOADES

The last word on this abysmal season goes to Ron Noades, who leaves us to wonder if he could possibly believe the patent nonsense he was talking when he declared: "I feel that the squad Alan Mullery and Ken Shellito have developed is capable of achieving our target for next season of promotion to Division One."

1983-84

It was obvious – even to Mullery – that the present squad would struggle again, albeit in a particularly poor Second Division, and his Summer clear-out meant the departure of Paul Hinshelwood, David Price, Ally Brown, Chris Jones, Tommy Langley, Ian Edwards and David Fry. Fry's replacement was Arsenal's George Wood, who was joined by some other experienced old professionals – John Lacy, Andy McCulloch and Les Strong. McCulloch was intended to partner Mabbutt in the forward line, but Mabbutt again sustained a serious injury – this time tearing his knee ligaments in a pre-season friendly – and wasn't able to play again until after Christmas. Mullery had also bought two other forwards, Tony Evans and Stan Cummins, but still found it necessary to take John Fashanu on loan, with a view to signing him permanently. At this time, Fashanu was very much in the shadow of his more famous brother (as were Hughton and Mabbutt) and after playing just two clumsy games for Palace he was sent back to Norwich. His reincarnation a couple of years later at Millwall surprised everyone, and not even Mullery's sternest critic could blame him for failing to spot a future England player.

GEORGE WOOD

The one new signing who did look particularly good was Stan Cummins, who his former manager Jackie Charlton had said – with his usual hyperbole – would one day play for England. He was certainly the best new player to arrive at the club since Kevin Mabbutt, but he suffered the same bad luck with injuries, only managing to play in fits and starts.

JOHN LACY

After a very slow beginning in the League, with only two points from five games, Palace could at least look forward to progressing beyond the first round of the League Cup, having comfortably beaten Peterborough 3-0 in the first leg. In the return game, however, Palace contrived to lose to the Fourth Division side by the same scoreline and were then knocked out on penalties, to earn themselves fines and a public scolding from Mullery. That outburst proved to be Mullery's most effective motivational act in his entire two years at Selhurst Park, because his team went on to win their next three league games, something unheard of since that famous victory against Ipswich – almost exactly four years earlier – and the ensuing hullabaloo.

The curious thing about Palace during this period was that they didn't seem to be playing to any recognisable plan, and were limping along from game to game relying more than ever on Vince Hilaire to make things happen. The success of Watford in Division One, and of Dave Bassett's Wimbledon team, was inspiring furious debate about the merits of the direct, long ball game, and upsetting the purists, but Mullery resisted adopting such tactics; he still believed that his ragged troops could carry on playing the passing game established by Venables, and in an attempt to recapture some of that former glory he brought Peter Nicholas back from Arsenal. The deal was an unusual, initially temporary arrangement, and Ron Noades appealed to the fans for money to finance the transfer. If they didn't quite dig into their pockets as he had hoped, at least most of them felt that Nicholas' return was exactly what was needed to bring about an improvement in results, but his influence was strangely negligible. He had obviously matured as a player whilst at Arsenal, but however well he played he couldn't raise the performance of his team mates sufficiently, and long before the end of the season it was clear that he had lost heart. Nicholas also missed a month of the season after being injured whilst playing for Wales, and at one stage so many of the first team squad were injured that debuts were given to two 17-year-olds, David Lindsay and Wayne Martin. This severely weakened team ended 1983 with just one point earned from seven games, and slipped from being fairly comfortable in the middle of the table towards the relegation area, above only Derby, Swansea and Cambridge.

As soon as Cannon, Nicholas and Mabbutt – arguably Palace's three best players – returned to the side, though, they started playing for the first time under Mullery with a bit of discipline and vigour, and the first few weeks of 1984 brought their best results of the entire season. The third round of the F.A.Cup paired Palace with First Division Leicester City, but the strike force of Gary Lineker and Alan Smith could find no way past Billy Gilbert – once again playing at his best – who then went on to put Palace through with the winning goal. They were drawn at home again in the next

round to West Ham, then occupying fourth place in Division One, and put up their best show yet to draw 1-1 in a game which they fully deserved to win. Sadly, Palace didn't play nearly so well in the replay a few days later and the Hammers won 2-0, but it was good to see a bit of self confidence creeping in. Similarly, in the League, there were two particularly pleasing results against Newcastle and Middlesborough. Newcastle had bought Kevin Keegan to help them win promotion, and their team also contained Terry McDermott, Peter Beardsley and Chris Waddle, so it was a surprise that Palace were such convincing 3-1 winners, and that they played so well. The next game, against Middlesborough, was always likely to be tough one, but was made even harder after both Gilbert and Mabbutt were sent off after 48 minutes. However, the nine remaining players did themselves proud, and the policy of passing to Vince Hilaire on the wing at every opportunity paid off when he was brought down for a penalty, from which Peter Nicholas scored the winner.

ANDY McCULLOCH

Just for a while it looked as though Mullery had at last got the machine working properly, but Mabbutt had come back from injury far too soon and was forced to miss a further two months of the season, which coincided with another slump in results. With Giles and McCulloch also injured, Alan Mullery's last signing for Palace – Phil Barber, bought from Aylesbury for £7,000 – was thrown into the team sooner than expected at the age of 19, briefly forming a lightweight partnership up front with Stan Cummins. He looked alright, but nothing special, and Palace ended another season with the usual problem remaining unsolved; that despite a sound defence, in which Gilbert had been outstanding, they simply couldn't score. For such an experienced striker, McCulloch's haul of four goals all season was pathetic, and the top scorer with seven goals – Tony Evans – had already been sold to Wolves.

TONY EVANS

Relegation had never really been a live possibility, but was only completely out of the question with two games to go, and Ron Noades was forced to accept, after two miserable years, that Alan Mullery really didn't have a clue. As soon as the season finished Noades sacked his fourth manager in as many years, and not a single tear was shed for the departing Mullery. A few days later the new manager was announced as Dave Bassett, the charmless cockney who had dragged Wimbledon up from the Fourth to the Second Division in successive seasons, and who clearly

had a talent for getting mediocre footballers to play to their strengths – surely the right man for the job at Palace! It was a big decision for Bassett to leave Wimbledon at such an exciting time, and he quickly realised it was the wrong one when he arrived at Selhurst Park and looked around him. Whatever horrors he saw left no doubt in his mind, and only four days after being appointed he turned straight round and went back to Plough Lane, leaving the Palace faithful more suspicious of Noades and his methods than ever. Inevitably, Malcolm Allison was one of the first names to be suggested as the new man at the top, along with Steve Kember, Brian Horton and Lou Macari, but in the end the surprising choice of Steve Coppell and Ian Evans delighted everyone. Coppell was still only 28 years old but his playing career had been truncated by injury, whilst Ian Evans was still massively popular with the fans, reminding them of happier times. In complete contrast to the reaction to Mullery's appointment, the Palace supporters were behind Coppell from the moment he came, because he had earned universal respect as a player, and as a spokesman for the P.F.A., of the kind that his predecessor never could.

1984-85

Steve Coppell had worn the No.7 shirt for Manchester United and England with great success, and it is not surprising that he was to see this position as a key one in rebuilding the team, signing the Scottish winger Alan Irvine from Everton. His assessment of where the weaknesses lay was spot on, and for the first time since the days of Kenny Sansom, Palace tried using a natural left back in the No.3 shirt, with Brian Sparrow coming from Arsenal. Trevor Aylott was signed from Luton as a direct replacement for McCulloch, and with Giles having gone during the Summer, Coppell signed another forward, Tony Mahoney from Brentford, although it never became clear what his position was meant to be. The really significant departures, of course, were Billy Gilbert and Vince Hilaire, whose contracts had expired and who were therefore at liberty to move wherever they wished. Inspired by Peter Nicholas' stated desire to leave the club, they at last decided to give up waiting for things to improve at Palace, and went to Portsmouth and Luton respectively, leaving an uncommitted Nicholas and Jerry Murphy

BRIAN SPARROW

behind, with Jim Cannon, as the last reminders of the halcyon days under Venables. With Gilbert gone, and Lacy of little use, Coppell signed Arsenal's central defender Chris Whyte, an excellent footballer who regrettably only played 17 games before returning to Highbury

under very peculiar circumstances.

At once the philosophical difference between Mullery and Coppell became evident, with the new manager's team starting from the premise of a solid and logical shape and players being used in very specific roles, contrasting with Mullery's confused and aimless formations.

TREVOR AYLOTT

Behind the scenes, Noades was claiming that the club was now heading in the right direction financially, denying accusations that Palace lacked ambition, although he did appeal for a millionaire to take over as Chairman and inject some cash for new players. He had in mind someone like Elton John, but the closest we got was a rumour about one of Status Quo, which came to nothing. Another good sign was that Alan Smith's youth team had been reconstituted, and two 15-year-olds – Richard Shaw and John Salako – were soon making names for themselves.

On the field, Coppell's newly wrought team made a poor start to the season, and very soon found themselves in the bottom three, with the manager fairly happy with his defence and midfield, but bemoaning "the age old problem of getting the ball in the onion bag". Trevor Aylott was carrying on where Langley, McCulloch, Jones and Brown had left off and

Mabbutt's by now predictable injury problem was once again keeping him out of the team, leaving Cummins and Mahoney to forage up front to little effect. Cummins, who had looked as if he could have been such a good player, was apparently homesick in London and moved back to Sunderland, and with Whyte moving back to Arsenal shortly afterwards, this gave Gavin Nebbeling an extended run in the centre of defence alongside Jim Cannon, who had by now passed Terry Long's club appearance record.

ALAN IRVINE

Apart from the perennial problem of scoring goals, the midfield formation was unbalanced, with Irvine, Stebbing and Nicholas all being exclusively right-sided players, and Murphy as the only left-footer. This was remedied when Phil Barber, who was bought originally as a centre forward, replaced Stebbing in the team and took up a position wide on the left, releasing Murphy to his more natural central position. The immediate effect was an unbeaten run of eight games, with the best result a 3-1 win at Grimsby, who had recently knocked Everton out of the League Cup, and who were one of the Second Division's better sides. Palace's second goal that night was scored by a player making the first League appearance of his career, the 20-year-old striker Andy

Gray, signed recently from Dulwich Hamlet. Gray had once been at Selhurst Park as a schoolboy, and had later joined Brentford as an apprentice before an ominous 'personality clash' with the manager seemed to put an end to his chances in the professional game. Coppell, still with little money to spend, had been scavenging around the local non-league teams for talent, and as well as cleverly spotting Gray's potential had also bought Steve Galloway from Sutton. Galloway did well in the reserves, scoring plenty of goals, but his way into the first team was blocked at first by Andy Gray, and ultimately by Ian Wright. Coppell was also persuaded to give a trial to Tony Finnigan – a friend of Gray's – and was sufficiently impressed to take him on as well, thus strengthening the squad at minimal cost.

The run of improved results came to an emphatic end when Palace lost 5-0 at Oxford, followed a few weeks later by a home defeat at the hands of Millwall in the League Cup and – especially humiliating – another 5-0 drubbing at home to Wimbledon, an abysmal performance which remains Palace's lowest point under Steve Coppell. His decisive response was to drop Nebbeling and Aylott, bringing in Stebbing and Finnigan in their places, but he knew that the main problem was a weakness in midfield caused by Peter Nicholas' acrimonious departure to Luton. Henry Hughton was a versatile player, having played in midfield, as centre back, right and left back, and even in goal when George Wood was injured against Shrewsbury, but he wasn't the answer to this particular problem. To fill the gap, Coppell spotted another bargain, and signed the undervalued Kevin Taylor from Derby. His inclusion in the team alongside Murphy restored the familiar symmetry to the midfield, but the signing that really proved to be Palace's short-term salvation was that of the giant centre half, Micky Droy from Chelsea. Despite his long experience in the First Division, not too many people expected very much from the 33-year-old, but he confounded everyone by transforming Palace's defence and emanating an aura of effortless self-confidence that settled all those around him. You simply knew that Droy would win everything in the air, and his trips forward for free kicks and corners – he scored in his first game – were reminiscent of Ian Evans at his troublesome best.

MICKY DROY

The most satisfying result for the few remaining fans was the 2-1 victory over Portsmouth which helped ruin the chances of Billy Gilbert and Vince Hilaire returning to Division One, and at the same time made Palace's own position fairly safe. By the end of the season they had climbed to 15th. in a 22-team division, well clear of relegation, and Coppell had started to lay the foundations for a successful future despite home crowds of frequently less than 5,000.

1985-86

When Jerry Murphy left Palace in the Summer of 1985, after being a regular in the team for the past seven seasons, he was still only 25 years old and should have been approaching his peak, so why he was allowed to go on a free transfer is a mystery, especially so since Coppell had at times managed to get him to play with a new robustness. Perhaps the manager saw that Murphy could never really supply the fighting qualities that were to become so important to his team in the long, hard slog out of the Second Division, or perhaps the player simply didn't fancy being forced to work so hard for his living. Along with Murphy went Tony Mahoney and – sadly – Kevin Mabbutt, whose latest attempt at a comeback had lasted just three full games, and who finally had to submit to repeated injury. Mahoney's replacement in the squad was a similarly anonymous left-sided forward called Andy Higginbottom, while Murphy's place went to Steve Ketteridge, who had looked particularly good when helping Wimbledon to destroy Palace the previous winter. The other player to come to Selhurst Park was yet another young, black non-league forward from a club few people had heard of – Ian Wright from Ten-Em-Bee – and Micky Droy was persuaded to postpone devoting himself to his second-hand car business for another year, signing a new contract for the season.

Palace quickly gave notice that they were at last coming good with some promising early league results, and a fine League Cup victory over Lennie Lawrence's expensively reconstructed Charlton side, who were on their way to Division One. The prize for beating Charlton was a second round draw against Coppell's old team, Manchester United, and he was justifiably proud of the way Palace played over the two legs, despite losing both games by a single goal. Although United's First Division class was obvious in both games, they were never allowed to take things easy for a moment, and the most significant effect on the Palace players was that they really

started to believe in their ability to work together as a team.

Ron Noades was also delighted with the home crowd of 21,506 – the best for two years – and gate receipts generally began to improve slightly as the season went on, although not enough to provide any more transfer money. Having stopped the financial rot, Ron Noades now came up with his latest brainchild for

STEVE KETTERIDGE

making money, not only for Palace, but for all participating clubs. 'Top Score' was a hideously complicated football pool to be operated by 86 of the 92 League clubs, and although few people thought it could ever work, Noades claimed that it would soon challenge the position of the major pools companies, the profit being ploughed back into the game. Typical of the scheme was the way that the Palace players – in the absence of any bona fide shirt sponsorship – sported a panel badly stitched onto their kit advertising Top Score and entreating the punters to "Play 6 from 49", a phrase which unsurprisingly failed to lodge itself in the consciousness of the nation; the competition finally folded after only three months.

With the emergence of Andy Gray as an unpredictable and dangerous goalscorer, and

Alan Irvine's steady supply of testing crosses from the right, Palace's style was now becoming geared towards relentless attack, and Phil Barber topped the Division Two scoring table by the end of August with six goals from the first five games. The defence had become rather leaky, though, with the two full back positions proving a bit of a problem for Coppell. He tried David Lindsay in place of Sparrow for a while, but then decided to

PAUL BRUSH

add some experience by buying Paul Brush from West Ham, relegating Sparrow to the odd appearance in midfield. Neither Hughton or Locke were entirely convincing at right back, and the young Irishman Ken O'Doherty was given a run at No.2, but whatever deficiencies there were in that position were compensated for by the fact that Cannon and Droy in the middle were as solid as any defensive partnership in the division. Being built like a munitions works, Droy rarely had to resort to foul play to win a challenge, but he was sent off in the home game against Millwall which, with Palace a goal behind, looked like resulting in their fourth defeat in five games. Not for the last time that season, though, Palace came from behind to win with goals from Barber and Gray, further evidence that Coppell had put some heart back into the team.

Three weeks after that Millwall game Palace once again found themselves trailing at home – this time 2-1 to Oldham – when Ian Wright came on as substitute for the ineffective Trevor Aylott. Wright had already scored several good goals for the reserves, but didn't yet look strong enough for the first team in his few appearances as substitute. His last-minute winning goal against Oldham, after Kevin Taylor's well hit equaliser, was headed in from such an unlikely position that it gave the impression of being a bit of a fluke. However, Wright was to score three more winning goals in the No.12 shirt throughout the rest of the season, and he quickly progressed from being "super-sub' to claim his place in the team alongside Andy Gray, a partnership that at its best was the most exciting I have seen.

KEVIN TAYLOR

With Kevin Taylor back in midfield after injury, Palace put together an excellent sequence of four wins and a draw in November, the highlight of which was a 3-1 victory at Leeds United. With neither Gray or Wright playing at Elland Road, Tony Finnigan alone was on the receiving end of the Yorkshire folk's traditional racism, but although he only scored three goals all season he saved two of them especially for that day, admitting that his anger at the crowd's behaviour had helped to fire him up.

Palace couldn't sustain the form to really challenge for promotion, and in particular were too often found wanting at home, losing to poor teams like Huddersfield, Hull and Shrewsbury, and more reasonably to Wimbledon and Norwich, after which they were never within spitting distance of the top three. By the last third of the season a good team pattern had emerged, with Finnigan dropping from midfield to right back, Nebbeling standing in very successfully for the injured Droy, and Irvine, Taylor, Ketteridge and Barber supplying Gray and Wright up front, Aylott finally having been dropped. The last month of the season saw the team earn some excellent results, once again putting paid to Portsmouth's ambitions by beating them 2-1, cruising to a 3-0 victory over Leeds, and

TONY FINNIGAN

putting four past Barnsley, Palace's best score for over three years. In fact the season's total of 57 League goals was the best since 1977, and from now on the fans could expect to see plenty of goals from Palace, whatever happened at the other end. The final position of fifth in the table was cause for celebration after so long spent struggling, and a year later would have earned Palace a place in the new play-off system for promotion, but Coppell was happy enough knowing that, by anyone's standards, he was succeeding as a manager.

Ron Noades chose a good time to announce the next money-making venture, with a new feeling of optimism on the terraces, and the

GARY STEBBING

Lifeline scheme was a success straight away. With half of the subscription money going back to members in the form of weekly prizes, they were happy to donate the rest to the club, whose solemn promise was that it would be used exclusively to buy new players; whether Palace's recent success can be directly attributed to Lifeline or not, at least that is how it is perceived. Of course, the more significant source of income was the rent obtained from Charlton Athletic, forced to share Selhurst Park after being sold out by their own directors, and despite which they were promoted to Division One as runners-up to Norwich. The only evidence of their presence was a portakabin tucked away in the corner of the ground, and while the arrangement made not a scrap of difference to the Palace fans, for the Valley faithful it was a rotten way to be treated. One hopes for their sakes that they can move back soon, however much Palace lose as a result.

Palace now found themselves in the unaccustomed position of being fancied for promotion, and that looked an accurate assessment when they won their first three games, two of them away from home. The first 'Lifeline' signing was the Millwall winger Anton Otulakowski, who immediately came into the team on the left, mirroring Irvine's role on the right. This meant Phil Barber reverting to centre forward and Andy Gray dropping to substitute, a strange decision since Gray had apparently established himself towards the end of the previous season, and combined particularly well with Wright. Coppell perhaps felt that Barber's graft was more valuable than Gray's erratic brilliance, and his selection of Phil Barber ahead of other, more gifted players is something for which he has been criticised ever since.

PHIL BARBER

Having only just scraped past Third Division Bury in the second round of the League Cup, Palace were once again drawn against First Division opposition – Brian Clough's Nottingham Forest – and relished the challenge after having done so well against Manchester United the year before. In fact they surpassed that performance in the home leg, drawing 2-2 after twice being ahead, and then lost the away leg by a single late goal from Clough's son. They really did play some excellent football

over the two games, and Forest could not have complained had Palace gone through to the next round rather than them.

Shortly after losing to Forest, Micky Droy went to Brentford on a free transfer and Gavin Nebbeling came back into the side, but the

MARK BRIGHT

most significant change was up front, with Mark Bright being signed from Leicester. Bright's first game was a dramatic affair against Ipswich, and he scored Palace's first goal on a day when Ian Wright's last-minute equaliser earned them a 3-3 draw, after an inexplicable run of five defeats had landed them back in the middle of the table. Soon afterwards, an injury to Otulakowski – from which he never recovered – allowed Barber back into the team on the left, and it was at the same time that Andy Gray began to stake his own claim for a midfield place, where his perverse talent was to eventually settle. Starting with a 5-1 destruction of Hull City, Palace embarked on a run of games that took them past Chistmas and into the New Year with five wins out of six, and once again they were back in contention at the top of the table. With confidence at a peak, the prospect of meeting Forest again in the F.A.Cup third round was one that they looked forward to without fear, and they played superbly to win by a single goal from Alan Irvine. Palace's £40,000 signing Gary O'Reilly made an impressive debut in this game, replacing Nebbeling, but the star for Palace was Tony Finnigan, a forward turned midfielder, turned right back, who now played the game of his life at left back to obliterate Forest's most dangerous

GARY O'REILLY

player, Franz Carr. Dreams of a glorious Cup run were swiftly shattered in the next round at White Hart Lane, though, when Spurs won easily by four goals, one of them a beautifully finished close range own goal from one of their former players, Gary O'Reilly.

The next few weeks were worrying ones for everyone connected with Palace, when it became known that the Wimbledon chairman, Sam Hammam, had approached Ron Noades with a view to merging the two clubs. All sorts of scenarios were invented, such as the two managers job-sharing, the names being combined, and only the best players from each team being kept on, but Noades disclaimed any such ideas, assuring anyone who believed him that all the moves had come from Hammam's direction. It later transpired that Steve Coppell was very much against any form of merger, but nevertheless Noades took the entirely honourable course of printing a questionnaire in the programme for the game against Blackburn, and promising to abide by

the opinion of the fans. With the results of the survey demonstrating the strength of feeling – the fans voting nine to one against a merger – the scheme was immediately scuppered, and the team celebrated by pummelling Birmingham 6-0. Gray's outstanding performance, coming through from midfield to score one and set up two other goals, finally sealed his place in the team at the expense of Ketteridge, who later moved on to that traditional home for old Palace players, Leyton Orient. From then on, Palace were always just outside the play-off positions, eventually missing out by one place, and in the final analysis it was again inconsistency at home that cost them the few crucial points, with earlier defeats by Shrewsbury and Grimsby being especially damaging.

ANDY GRAY

It was interesting, after the 0-0 draw with Plymouth, that Steve Coppell drew attention to their uncomplicated long-ball game, and contrasted it with what he saw as Palace's more subtle approach through midfield. The polarisation of opinion on this issue over the last few years has now become such that too many commentators on the game start from the point of putting a team into one category or another, and let that dictate how they go about watching the game. Palace themselves have fallen foul of this lazy approach, becoming branded as 'Route One' merchants, when in fact Coppell's teams have always placed great importance on the use of wingers, and have been most effective when first Irvine, then Redfearn, then McGoldrick have been on song. It may be true that the defenders have on the whole lacked the ability of someone like Alan Hansen to bring the ball forward, but that isn't the same thing at all as the gung-ho tactics so favoured by Wimbledon, and so despised elsewhere.

The last home match of the season had all the makings of a great game, with Palace wanting to win to give themselves a chance of making the play-offs, and Portsmouth needing victory to go up as champions. With Gilbert and Hilaire once again on the opposing side, the biggest crowd of the season witnessed Palace outplay Pompey and win with a goal from substitute John Salako, although Ian Wright's final touch gave him the credit. As it turned out, Portsmouth still went up and Palace stayed down, but the result emphasised that at their best Palace could match anyone in the Second Division, and would surely be the team to catch in next year's race for promotion.

1987-88

This was the season that Palace really became a joy to watch, and the crowds came back accordingly, largely thanks to the emergence of Mark Bright and Ian Wright as truly great goalscorers. Having failed narrowly to make the play-offs the previous season it was surprising that Coppell chose to sell two such important team members as Alan Irvine and Kevin Taylor, the former going to Dundee United and the latter to Scunthorpe after his wife apparently insisted on moving back up north. Their replacements, however, succeeded in improving the team significantly, and illustrated Coppell's ability to spot talented players from the lower divisions. The more expensive of the two was Neil Redfearn, costing £85,000 from Doncaster, but it was Geoff Thomas, a £55,000 signing from Crewe Alexandra who was to prove such a bargain. Neither of them had any trouble adapting to the higher grade and they slotted into the team's established pattern with ease.

After a couple of shaky draws and a defeat at Barnsley, Palace struck a seam of form that lifted them, after seven games, to the top of the division. The most spectacular victory was in the game at Birmingham, who Palace once again beat 6-0, and perhaps the best performance came in the 4-1 defeat of West Bromwich Albion. Mark Bright was now the top scorer in Division Two, with eight goals in six games, but the most promising aspect of Palace's game was the midfield partnership of Andy Gray and Geoff Thomas, both playing with great confidence, constantly spraying the ball out wide to Redfearn and Salako and getting it forward to Wright and Bright. With Thomas running non-stop to win posession, Gray was given a lot of freedom to get forward and this first part of the season produced the most consistently dynamic and exhilarating football seen for a long while. Just when things were going so well Palace were knocked back, first by injury, and then by internal strife. After beating Reading 3-2, Palace suddenly found themselves without the services of five

defenders; Brush, Finnigan, Stebbing and O'Reilly all had long term injuries while Jim Cannon was forced to miss four games, his first absence from the team for over three years. With a makeshift back four of O'Doherty, Nebbeling, Thomas and young Richard Shaw, Palace lost their next two games, against Ipswich and – inevitably – Shrewsbury, although they easily overcame Newport County over two legs in the League Cup.

GAVIN NEBBELING

More destructive was the fact that Andy Gray's opinion of his own worth had now expanded to the point where he made it known that he had outgrown Crystal Palace, and in effect invited bigger clubs to come and get him, which Aston Villa's Graham Taylor duly did. Although Coppell wanted to keep such an obviously talented player, the turmoil which Gray caused to team morale was intolerable, and Coppell was ultimately glad to get shot of him. It transpired that Jim Cannon in particular could not abide Gray's arrogance, and whether the tales of them coming to blows are true or not, it is not hard to imagine. According to some stories, George Wood was also involved in whatever was going on, and it is interesting that within six months all three players had left the club. The sale of Gray for the absurdly low fee of £150,000 left a gap in midfield that was never adequately filled, and I maintain that had the partnership of Gray and Thomas stayed intact, then Palace would have won promotion that year, although I have no doubt

GLENN PENNYFATHER

that Coppell did the right thing at the time. The player bought to replace Gray, for the same amount of money, was Southend's Glenn Pennyfather; a busy grafter who lacked inspiration, Pennyfather shared the position for the rest of the season with another hard working but unspectacular player, the former Yeovil part-timer Alan Pardew.

A more successful purchase was that of left back David Burke from Huddersfield, and with Stebbing replacing the disappointing O'Doherty at right back, Palace settled down once again to record six wins from seven games, which put them back into contention in fourth place. The first game of that run was against Plymouth, with Andy Gray making his penultimate appearance and playing a major part in the 5-1 victory; the hero, though, was Ian Wright, who became Palace's first hat-trick scorer since Mike Flanagan in 1980. Once again Palace were drawn against Manchester United in the League Cup at Old Trafford, and despite going two down pulled a goal back through O'Doherty, and again

pleased Coppell by looking the better side for much of the game.

The most dramatic match of the season was the one at Maine Road, where Palace won 3-1 after the Manchester City goalkeeper Eric Nixon was sent off, and Mark Bright scored two goals but came away with a broken arm, which kept him out for the next six games. Bright was still injured for the next game, against his old team Leicester, but after being 3-1 up Palace threw the game away to draw 4-4; the blame was put squarely on the shoulders of George Wood, who had recently been criticised by the fans for giving away several vital goals, and who only played once more before moving to Cardiff. His final game was against Newcastle in the F.A.Cup, where Palace were knocked out by a goal from the latest Geordie sensation Paul Gascoigne, despite controlling most of the game. Gascoigne had not yet become a demi-god, and was still mortal flesh, although plenty of it.

PERRY SUCKLING

With Wood ruthlessly dropped from the team, Coppell went out and spent £100,000 on Perry Suckling, Manchester City's reserve keeper, who immediately reduced the number of goals conceded, keeping Palace on the edge of the promotion race until the very last game of the season. They also qualified for a half-baked tournament at Wembley to mark the League's centenary, and although they were knocked out on penalties by Sheffield Wednesday it at least gave the players probably the only chance of playing at Wembley that they would ever get.

belonged. That Steve Coppell had turned Palace into a club deserving of the loyalty of such players is testament both to his skills as a manager and his personal qualities.

DAVID BURKE

Palace approached the last few games with the final play-off place still in their sights; after beating Blackburn 2-0, with Perry Suckling saving a penalty from Steve Archibald, and losing 1-0 at Leeds, they knew exactly what was needed from the final game at home to Manchester City. If Palace could win, then the champions Millwall only needed to force a draw at home to Blackburn for Palace to qualify for the play-offs. Nebbeling headed Palace into the lead from Burke's free kick, and then Thomas' second goal sent the crowd into ecstasy when word got around that Millwall had drawn level at The Den. In reality the Lions had lost 4-1, and by all accounts seem to have taken things very easy indeed, although nobody has dared to make the obvious accusation. For the third year running Palace had just missed out, and the great worry was that Bright and Wright – who had scored an astonishing 48 goals between them – would surely be tempted to make their own way directly to Division One, where they clearly

1988-89

To find Jim Cannon's name missing from the team sheet after 15 years took some getting used to, but was no great surprise. He could have probably played on for another year or so, but Coppell's ambitions for Crystal Palace required him to take a longer-term view, and improve each position wherever possible. Many people felt that Cannon was badly treated, but Coppell had shown his ruthless streak before – in the case of George Wood – and knew that he had to replace parts before they were worn out. The fans' loyalty to, and affection for Cannon made it difficult for the new man to win them over, but Jeff Hopkins - for whom Palace paid £250,000 to Fulham - undoubtedly improved the team and eventually did a grand job as captain at the end of the season.

JEFF HOPKINS

Less easy to understand was the release of Tony Finnigan to Blackburn, because although Palace had bought John Pemberton as a specialist right back, Finnigan had proved himself more than reliable in all sorts of positions and would have been extremely useful later on in midfield. To cover that area, Coppell had bought Dave Madden, who together with Pardew looked destined for the reserves, but who ended up as one of the heroes the following Spring.

Palace were reasonably pleased with their first result, a 1-1 draw with the eventual champions Chelsea, but with Nebbeling injured and Hopkins serving a suspension, Geoff Thomas was forced back into defence for the second game, a 2-0 defeat at home to Watford. Pardew thus came into the midfield with Pennyfather, and although he would never have been first choice he managed to stay there for virtually the rest of the season. Watford's victory was a quite convincing one, and for a few months they looked certain to bounce straight back to Division One; in the end they finished a place behind Palace in fourth, and lost out in the play-offs, demonstrating what a very long season it is in the Second Division nowadays.

By the time of the next game, against Walsall, both Glenn Pennyfather and Perry Suckling had been forced out with injuries, but Brian Parkin was an able deputy in goal, and with Hopkins and O'Reilly now back together in central defence, Thomas was again able to move forward into the midfield. Coppell's indecision about his wingers continued with Barber soon winning back his place from Salako, who in turn frequently came on as substitute for Redfearn, who began to feel aggrieved.

After six league games, Palace had yet to win, were in 20th. position, and even Mark Bright hadn't scored a goal; perhaps Cannon's leadership had been more important to the well being of the team than Coppell had realised. Then, for no apparent reason, everything clicked into place and Palace won seven of their next eight games, including both legs of the League Cup tie against Swindon, and a 4-1 defeat of Plymouth which Palace so dominated that they could easily have scored ten. The one defeat came at Ewood Park, where after apparently cruising to another three points they managed to lose 5-4 to Blackburn, beginning the persistent worries about the frail nature of Palace's defence.

Despite Redfearn's important part in Palace's revival, he was still miffed at being substituted in earlier games, and Steve Coppell reluctantly granted his transfer request, whilst making it clear that he didn't want him to go. It seemed peculiar behaviour by Redfearn at the time,

NEIL REDFEARN

and I wonder whether he now regrets throwing away the chance of making it to the First Division, having failed to get there since with either Watford or Oldham. Into Redfearn's place came Alex Dyer, recently bought from Hull, for whom he had played especially well in recent games against Palace. It was intended that Dyer should play wide on the left, but he filled the gap on the right wing until Eddie McGoldrick's arrival, and his five goals in as many games included one direct from a corner to beat Birmingham, before injury put him out for the rest of the season. Also ruled out from then on was Geoff Thomas, who had justified the decision to appoint him as captain in only his second year, but whose insistence on maximum physical exertion for every minute of every game put him into hospital for a hernia operation. Pennyfather came back into midfield, and with two thirds of the season gone Palace were still nicely placed within three points of the play-offs, and poised for the run-in, as well as nearly reaching Wembley in the Full Members Cup, now called the Simod Cup. After knocking out Walsall,

Southampton, Luton and Middlesborough – winning this last game 3-2 after being 2-1 down with two minutes left – Palace had to travel to Nottingham Forest for the semi-final, and were not disgraced in losing 3-1 after David Burke was harshly sent off.

After this, their league form stuttered slightly, with Bournemouth inflicting only the second home defeat of the season, and it looked as though Palace had blown it once again, dropping below half way in the table. The turning point came at Vicarage Road, with Barber's superbly taken goal wreaking revenge on Watford, and a run of nine wins from eleven games put Palace right back into contention at the top. Come the final game of the season they still had a slim chance of grabbing the second automatic promotion place from Manchester City, the equation being that Palace needed to win by five goals against Birmingham, and City had to lose at Bradford. Palace were in rampant, irresistible form, but a large number of drunks had come down in fancy dress to celebrate Birmingham's relegation, and not only ruined the day but – which was worse – acted as if they hadn't even noticed the appalling carnage at Hillsborough a few weeks earlier, the inevitable result of the hooliganism of the last two decades. With fights having started in a part of the New Stand, a number of others broke through the recently lowered barriers and staged a full-scale pitch invasion, complete with the pathetic parody of combat so beloved of British youth. The cavalry arrived after what seemed like an age and broke up the proceedings with ease, allowing the game to continue. Although the blame mostly goes to a small number of the visiting supporters, there were enough home fans relishing getting involved to make one thoroughly sick and ashamed. The sad truth is that no legislation can prevent the barely concealed macho instincts of the young male from surfacing with the slightest excuse.

With order restored, Ian Wright completed a

hat-trick, and Palace's domination of the game was such that they could certainly have won by more than 4-1, but the delay meant that the result from Bradford was known long before the end; a draw meant that Manchester City had finished just a point ahead of Palace, and the disappointed players saw out the bulk of the second half without too much strenuous effort.

RUDI HEDMAN

At last, after three years of coming so close, Palace had made it to the play-offs, and approached them confident in the knowledge that they had finished a clear third in the table, and simply deserved promotion. With both O'Reilly and Nebbeling injured, the latest signing – Rudi Hedman – was thrown in at the deep end, and played his part in a decidedly dodgy defence, although it was Jeff Hopkins whose own goal gave Swindon the advantage in the first leg of the semi-final. It was fitting that Bright and Wright should score the two goals in the home leg which won the tie, and put Palace through to the final against Blackburn. One of the worst defensive performances of the season had been in the earlier 5-4 defeat at Ewood Park, and once again Palace were prone to some alarming errors at the back, Blackburn this time winning 3-1; even the to the most optimistic fan, it was now hard to fancy Palace to come back in the

second leg. Nevertheless, a capacity crowd of 30,000 turned up at Selhurst Park to give them a final push, and the atmosphere surpassed even that of the Burnley game ten years earlier, with the task apparently that much more difficult and the tension palpable. Steve Coppell had a crucial decision to make, because both of his injured centre backs were now fit again, and his choice of O'Reilly rather than Nebbeling precipitated the latter's angry demand for a transfer. As it turned out, O'Reilly played out of his skin alongside Hopkins, and Palace's triumph was built on a defence that looked safer than it had all season. Alan Pardew had still not been accepted by the crowd despite his undeniable improvement throughout the season, but the pass which he made with the outside of his right foot to set up Ian Wright's first goal was a touch of genius which transformed him overnight into a cult hero. Wright himself reacted instinctively to the half chance to make it 1-0, and Palace were steaming.

EDDIE McGOLDRICK

In the second half Eddie McGoldrick received the ball and set off on a diagonal run towards the goal, which was something he had been oddly reluctant to try, considering his status as the Coppellite winger of the side. McGoldrick ran out of steam and lost control of the ball as he came inside the penalty area, but defender

Mark Atkins bundled him down anyway, and George Courteney pointed without hesitation to the penalty spot for the most peculiar and unnecessary offence I have ever seen. Back in March, Palace had been awarded four penalties in a game against Brighton and only scored one: since then the job had been successfully given to the player now wearing the No.4 shirt, the transfer-listed Dave Madden. Although he was obviously Coppell's fourth

DAVE MADDEN

choice in midfield behind Thomas, Pennyfather and Pardew, Madden had got better and better since being given his chance, and the crowd really appreciated a player who could consistently make space and time for himself to look up and make long, accurate passes to his colleagues. Madden it was, then, who kept his cool to put Palace 2-0 ahead from the spot, levelling the aggregate scores and taking the game to extra time. After another half-hour's play, that scoreline would have been enough for Palace to win, with the away goal counting double, but Ian Wright's simple header near the end from McGoldrick's cross made it 3-0, and put Palace once again back into Division One. That game had many heroes, but the one who deserves particular praise is Perry Suckling. With the score still at 2-0, Blackburn's admirable Simon Garner struck the best shot of the game, a perfect volley

from the edge of the box, but Suckling made a first class save to tip it over the bar, and ruin what was perhaps Garner's best ever chance to make it to where he belonged, in the First Division.

To have missed out on promotion for a fourth time might have been so disheartening for Palace that it could have left the club in crisis, and certainly both Bright and Wright would have been strongly tempted to move on, but the emphatic way that the team overcame both Swindon and Blackburn after being behind was an indication of the quality that they had above all others; their spirit. Coppell had assembled a collection of good and average players, the sum of which was greater than its parts, and nobody could deny that they deserved their chance in the First Division, although most also thought that their stay would be a brief one. To be a Palace fan that day felt wonderful; at 3 o'clock we were more or less resigned to applauding a brave but doomed effort, and by 5.15 we were celebrating with all the passion that had been unspent for the past ten years.

1989-90

The dilemma that Steve Coppell faced as he made his preparations for life at the top was whether he should stay loyal to the players who had earned promotion, or strengthen the team in the areas where it was obviously weak. Taking a dispassionate view, most fans would have agreed that Phil Barber and Alan Pardew – for all their dedication – were not likely to be up to the task, and many also had doubts about the defence, particularly David Burke and Jeff Hopkins. Coppell largely agreed with that assessment, buying Mark Dennis and Andy Gray from Q.P.R. to replace Burke and Pardew, and trusting that Alex Dyer would at last be fit to take over on the left wing from Barber. Curiously, though, he didn't see fit to invest in another centre back, which meant a lack of cover in that position since the departure of Gavin Nebbeling; this proved a big problem once O'Reilly was injured, and forced Geoff Thomas to stand in, with mixed results.

The decision to bring Andy Gray back to Selhurst Park was a brave one by Coppell, who knew that it would be seen as eating humble pie, after taking such an apparently principled stand when he sold Gray less than two years before. On top of this was the fact that he cost Palace more than three times what Villa had paid, but Coppell couldn't resist restoring the Gray / Thomas / Bright / Wright combination, and I for one agreed with him wholeheartedly. As it turned out, Gray and Thomas only played three games together in central midfield before Thomas was used first in defence, then wide on the left, after which Gray played the second half of the season on the right wing. Some would say that it was foolhardy of Coppell to give Mark Dennis another chance to resurrect his career, but we were never given much opportunity to judge whether or not he had become a reformed character, injury keeping him out of the side for all but nine mid-season games.

The season started with an unattractive fixture away to Q.P.R., and although Palace played

reasonably well they were beaten fair and square by Trevor Francis' team, the main disappointment being the failure to score. The next game was at home to Manchester United in midweek, Ian Wright's well struck late goal after Alex Dyer's flick on earning Palace a draw against a United side already being touted as title contenders after their impressive victory over the champions Arsenal. Palace in fact played much better in their third game, at home to Coventry, but were taught a lesson in how to kill a game stone dead by their defensive opponents, whose 1-0 win was completely undeserved.

STEVE COPPELL

The prognosis, then, was worrying; three games played, one goal scored, and only one point. Luckily, their next opponents – Wimbledon – were absolutely awful, and perhaps the ease of the 2-0 victory deceived the players into thinking rather more of themselves than was warranted, and was certainly no sort of preparation for the devastation to come at Anfield, just two days later. According to Steve Coppell, Palace created more chances that night than they had in any game so far, and Geoff Thomas even missed a penalty, but it seemed that whenever Liverpool came forward they scored a goal, which happened nine times. My knowledge of the game is all second hand, because I haven't yet been able to bring myself to watch the rush-released video of the game, but the concensus seems to be that many other teams have played worse at Anfield and got away with losing 3-0 or 4-0. If Liverpool's performance will go down in history, then so will the behaviour of Palace's travelling fans that night, who took their team's humiliation with humour and a strange sort of pride. The best joke was the chant; "You're not singing any more", directed at the empty Kop end after the stadium had been cleared of Liverpudlians, and although Coppell said that "This will haunt us for the rest of our lives", the fans who were there made sure that they would look back on that night with affection.

Up to that point the defence had looked competent enough, but now Coppell was under intense pressure to make improvements, with poor Perry Suckling bearing the brunt of the criticism, unfairly in the view of many. With few alternatives available to him in defence, Coppell had little choice but to name an unchanged side for the next game, and they showed extraordinary character to bounce back in the way that they did, pushing Southampton all the way to earn a 1-1 draw. That result was overlooked by Palace's critics, who had now written them off as certain to be relegated at the end of the season, but the players confounded everyone with their next two results – victories over Nottingham Forest and Everton – which pushed them into the top half of the table. Those two games saw them playing with a confidence and discipline that nobody would have believed possible a couple of weeks earlier, and they maintained their impetus against Millwall, coming back from Hopkins' farcical own goal to win 4-3, with Bright and Wright scoring two goals each and looking at their buoyant best.

This surge of good form reached a peak in their next game, when they met Nottingham Forest in the third round of the League Cup, having narrowly negotiated the previous round

over two dramatic legs against Leicester. Palace completely outplayed Forest – the eventual winners of the trophy – but just couldn't get the goal they deserved, which is why it was so hard to believe that they could have lost the replay as heavily as they did, by 5-0. Having defended his goalkeeper until now, Coppell had to concede that Suckling's loss of confidence was permeating the entire defence, and when he let in three more goals just three days later, it was the final straw. Suckling was replaced by Brian Parkin for the next game, ostensibly with a hand injury, and then Palace finally got the man they had been thinking about for a long time – the first million-pound goalkeeper, Nigel Martyn. Palace fans were deeply divided about Martyn at first, many thinking that a million pounds could be better spent in other areas, and believing that the popular Suckling had been unfairly treated. Such misgivings were reinforced when Martyn let eight goals past

NIGEL MARTYN

him in his first three league games, barely managing a save of any note. Perhaps the worst performance of the season came at home to Q.P.R., when the superannuated midfielders Peter Reid and Ray Wilkins were given as much time and space as they could wish for, and the recent, belated dismissal of Trevor Francis as manager inspired them to a decisive 3-0 win.

Now down once again to 18th. position, prospects again looked bleak, when Coppell finally made the signing that everyone had been clamouring for, that of a good centre

ANDY THORN

half. Andy Thorn was the player needed to firm up the defence, and he immediately looked the part in his first game, away to Manchester United. Playing five at the back for the first time, Palace didn't gain many friends, but they did register their first away win of the season against all the odds, and this proved to be a turning-point, after which Palace always managed to keep themselves just clear of the relegation places. There were some more bad results – in particular at Arsenal and Everton – but also some convincing victories over Southampton, Spurs and Aston Villa, and survival was comfortably secured with three games still to be played. In fact, were it not for Manchester City's last minute equaliser in the final game of the season, after Niall Quinn had clearly controlled the ball with his hand, Palace would have finished the season in 12th. place in Division One – their highest ever.

If there had been no more to Palace's season than that, it would still have been just cause for celebration, bearing in mind the low expectations at the outset: but of course this was also the year that Crystal Palace reached the F.A.Cup final, for the first time in their

history. For the record, let us also remember that for the second year running Palace reached the last four of the Full Members / Simod / Zenith Data Systems Cup, cruising past Luton, Charlton and – eventually – Swindon, before falling apart against Chelsea, who went on to win the final. The other route to Wembley had been less challenging up to that point, at least on paper, and Palace certainly had the luck of the draw. They entered the F.A.Cup in the third round, and made heavy weather of despatching Second Division strugglers Portsmouth. Nigel Martyn in the Palace goal was at fault as Guy Whittingham's looped header put Pompey ahead, and it took a cracking volley from Geoff Thomas to put his team back in the game. With time running out, and the match heading for a replay on the South coast, Andy Gray found himself just outside the Portsmouth box with the ball at his feet, and instantly decided to win a penalty. He pushed the ball forward past Mark Chamberlain, who obligingly stuck out a leg for Gray to trip over, slowly pick himself up and thump home the resulting spot kick.

The next round was somewhat easier, as it should have been against an awfully poor Huddersfield defence, and although Ian Wright was missing after breaking his leg in a league game against Liverpool – just as he was about to score – Palace should still have got more than the four they managed, courtesy of Hopkins, Salako, Bright and a messy own goal. Rewarded with another home tie in the fifth round against Fourth Division Rochdale, Palace were nearly thwarted by a series of stunning saves by goalkeeper Paul Welch, who was only beaten by Barber's firm right foot shot from close range. Having hit the winner, Barber reeled away triumphantly towards his chief critics in the New Stand enclosure who had been getting on his back after his recent form, which had been undeniably bad. With only eight teams left in the competition, Palace were once again given nearly the best draw possible against another

Fourth Division side, this time away at Cambridge. One always had a feeling that this would be a difficult one, though, and Cambridge played the better football for much of the game; but Palace never panicked and finally won with a scrappy goal, weakly directed into the net by Geoff Thomas' normally redundant right foot.

With due respect to Palace's opponents, few teams can ever have had such an easy passage to the semi-finals, and everyone watched the live draw for the next round praying to be paired with Oldham, or at a pinch Manchester United, but definitely, definitely not Liverpool. We got Liverpool, and we knew that we were in for another onslaught of sneering reminders of the 9-0 scoreline back in September. The more recent league game, however, had offered some small encouragement to the more optimistic among us, because Palace were never overrun, and might even have snatched a draw. With Liverpool 1-0 up in that game, Palace nevertheless came back into it and almost scored when Ian Wright took the ball swiftly past Grobbelaar, only for Barry Venison to save a certain goal with a blocking tackle that – it turned out – broke Wright's leg. He hobbled on for a while, but when McGoldrick was fouled, Coppell took the opportunity to replace him and Pardew with the two substitutes; a rash move, since McGoldrick was also badly injured, and Palace were left with ten men for the last 20 minutes. The final score of 2-0 at least illustrated how far Palace had come since the start of the season, and with Ian Wright having recovered in time for the Cambridge game, they felt that they would be able to put up a decent fight in the semi-final, even if it was now more improbable than ever that they would be going to Wembley this year. After Ian Wright had broken his leg for a second time, a victim of his own skill in turning wickedly past a Derby defender, any chance of upsetting the champions elect had – according to every expert they could dig up – completely vanished,

and the semi-final was now seen as nothing more than Liverpool's chance for a bit of target practice before completing the inevitable double.

Executives of television companies now dictate the fixture list for Cup as well as league games, so for the first time both semi-finals were to be played on a Sunday, one at noon and the other at 3.30, for the benefit of the T.V. audience. The Football Association, determined to prove beyond all doubt their incompetence, scheduled the local derby between Manchester United and Oldham for 3.30 at Maine Road, meaning that the other two sets of fans had to make their way from Liverpool and London to Aston Villa's ground in Birmingham, with orders to arrive by 11 in the morning. I am ashamed to say that I didn't bother going, being convinced that a long journey up would be followed by a longer one home, after a noble 1-0 defeat. My decision was also influenced by memories of the terrible anti-climax of losing the semi-final in 1976, and of course by the fact that I could see the game live on the box anyway.

A room full of us settled down to watch the game hoping for the best and fearing the worst, and were surprised how calm and confident our team looked, in the biggest game of their lives. For the first time all season they were taking their time on the ball and passing it around at the back, in fact doing exactly what Liverpool do when they are sitting on a lead. Coppell's tactic was to contain Liverpool for the first half and then have a go at them later on, and to this end he detailed Pemberton to stick to Barnes, O'Reilly to Rush, and Shaw to Houghton, orders which they carried out to perfection. Then, out of the blue, McMahon gave the ball to Pardew, who gave it straight back, and McMahon's through pass caught O'Reilly coming forward, leaving Rush clear to place a precise shot past Martyn. That goal was all that separated the teams during the first half, but Palace stayed calm, stuck to their plan, and went into the break pleased with having played every bit as well as Liverpool. John Motson, the world's most aggravating commentator, was watching a different game, and Ray Wilkins didn't have the wit to depart from his prepared script, the gist of which was that Liverpool are majestic: "Majestic", he proclaimed of their complete control of the game. And Alan Hansen? Well, he was just "majestic – I can't think of any other word !". How these people get paid for spouting so much drivel, I have no idea. Ironically, the one pundit to look at the game objectively was Terry Venables, whose fair and intelligent comments may have bought him some forgiveness from those who call him Judas, not that he could care less.

As Liverpool kicked off the second half, they were quietly confident of the course of the next 45 minutes, but as John Pemberton quickly

JOHN PEMBERTON

intercepted the ball, someone lit his fuse and let him go. He skinned two Liverpool defenders – which you simply don't do – and belted a cross towards the head of Barber. It fell to Salako, whose fierce shot hit Grobbelaar, looped into the air and was blasted into the net by Bright for the equaliser. If we went potty then, we went even pottier when Gary O'Reilly forced the ball in from close range to put

Palace – unbelievably – in front, and for a while it looked as though they would hold on to the 2-1 lead, so well were they playing. Then McMahon equalised after an extremely dubious free kick, and minutes later Liverpool went ahead again, this time following an equally dubious penalty decision, Barnes scoring from the spot. Having regained the lead so emphatically, the natural response was to assume that this time Liverpool would hold on tight, and after the earlier ecstasy we couldn't help but think that now it was all over, gallant though the effort had been. Andy Gray's equalising goal, when it came, epitomised the difference between the two teams that day, with Geoff Thomas twice getting first to the ball and heading it goalwards, and then Gray outjumping the besieged Liverpool defenders to head firmly into the net. Palace had put themselves back into the game again by displaying the same sense of purpose and solidarity that had earned promotion the year before, and 90 minutes of pure drama came to a climax with Andy Thorn heading against the bar, when he looked certain to score the winner.

Another half an hour's play was ahead of us, and logic decreed that Palace's novices could surely not withstand Liverpool's superior fitness, experience and skill in this unknown territory. Certainly the pace slowed, but Palace defended superbly, given strength by Nigel Martyn's assurance in goal, and a replay seemed on the cards until Alan Pardew's late, unforgettable and frankly preposterous winner. The corner played hard to the near post has become the vogue in recent years, and this one looked like an illustration from a coaching manual; Thorn flicked Gray's corner across the box and away from the goalkeeper, and Pardew popped up between two defenders needing only the slightest contact to convert the goal for which that player will always be famous. What had been the most astonishing and exciting game of football in recent memory had been witnessed by millions on television, but those fans who had travelled up to the Midlands were privileged to be a part of the most intense, emotional and unreal day in Palace's history. All I could do at home was scream with joy as the final whistle went, knowing that the team I loved had beaten the nation's finest 4-3, and were in the Cup Final. How good it felt being a Palace fan for the

ALAN PARDEW

next day and the next few weeks; all sorts of unlikely people offered congratulations as if you had scored the winning goal yourself, and so many said that it was the best game they had ever seen that you couldn't help almost bursting with pride. What made it perfect was that Palace utterly deserved to win, and everyone except that prize bore Jimmy Hill – who preferred to blame Bruce Grobbelaar – recognized the fact. The last word on the semi-final is that the score between Crystal Palace and Liverpool that most people will recall is not 9-0, but 4-3.

Opinion was sharply divided on who Palace would prefer as their opponents at Wembley - the Second Division giant-killers Oldham, a team with a similar spirit to Palace's, or the ragged collection of over-priced individuals known as Manchester United. After United had unconvincingly whinged their way past the Latics, Palace were confident that the cup was theirs for the taking, having already beaten

and drawn with United in the league, and finished the season on the same number of points. The big question leading up to the final was whether Ian Wright would be back in time from his second broken leg, and it was only during the final week before the game that he had his first 90-minute run-out in a reserve game. Andy Thorn was in danger of missing out for a while, but made a spectacular recovery from a badly injured heel, and Mark Dennis, Jeff Hopkins, Alex Dyer and Eddie McGoldrick were all fighting to be fit in time. The other talking point was the patently unjust allocation of tickets by the F.A., which resulted in Palace having only 14,000 out of 80,000 available seats in the ground, with Manchester United's quota nearly double that. Confusion reigned, with Ron Noades on the one hand laying into the F.A., ostensibly on the fans' behalf, and on the other hand making sure that he realised the maximum revenue by allowing those with enough money to effectively buy themselves priority. The arguments about the fairest way of allocating Palace's share of the tickets could go on for ever, but I can see no reasonable opposition to the notion of giving top priority to existing Club members, in recognition of their loyalty.

The town of Croydon was festooned with red and blue, and everywhere you went you would see Palace shirts, thousands of people having paid over £20 for the honour of walking around advertising Virgin Airlines. The prospect of Palace meeting and maybe beating United seemed to excite the rest of the country as well, and it became the most eagerly awaited Cup Final for many, many years. Although United have an amazing number of supporters throughout the world, everyone else was rooting for Palace, and when it came to the day itself we certainly didn't feel like the underdogs the bookmakers claimed we were.

The atmosphere at Wembley was simply wonderful, and with no hint of trouble from rival fans it just felt that you were part of a great old-fashioned sporting occasion, with a cloth cap and a rattle. As the players came on to the pitch, the cascade of red and blue balloons from the Palace section made a display of colour that the T.V. cameras couldn't hope to do justice to, and the club's biggest moment in 85 years had arrived. With Ian Wright on the substitutes' bench, the team who started the game were the same 11 men who had seen off Liverpool, and once again it was clear that Coppell had decided to retain the man-for-man marking system that had been so effective in that game. Richard Shaw stuck closely to Neil Webb, and with John Salako more or less at left back, Mark Bright was left alone up front with support on the wings coming from

JOHN SALAKO

Barber and Gray. It was no surprise that the first goal should come from a free kick planted high into the penalty area, since all the experts had latched on to the fact that all four Palace goals in the semi-final had come from such free kicks or corners. Gray feinted, Barber crossed, and O'Reilly's header squeezed away from between him and Pallister and looped over the flapping Jim Leighton into the net. Palace tried desperately to hang on to the lead for the rest of the half, but a clear foul by Bruce on Gray gave possession to United, and the defence stood and watched as Wallace and McClair combined to set up Robson for the

headed equaliser, although the decisive touch came from John Pemberton's shin. That mishap aside, Palace had defended well, making at least as many chances as Manchester United, and went in at half-time still feeling confident that they would win.

The second half continued along the same lines until another bit of lax defending by Palace presented a chance to Mark Hughes, who had done little up to that point, but who snapped it up to put United 2-1 ahead. Steve Coppell delayed the inevitable substitution until 20 minutes from the end, but when Ian Wright eventually came on, the effect was devastating. With his very first touch of the game he got away from Phelan's lunge, left Pallister on his backside in the box, and stroked the ball past Leighton for one of the most perfect goals he will ever score. The game had swung Palace's way, but with players already dropping with cramp they were just unable to press home their advantage in normal time, although Gray came extremely close with a right foot shot on the turn, and another half an hour of a classic Cup Final was needed.

The game was barely two minutes into extra time when Geoff Thomas chipped an exquisite ball through to Salako, who wheeled away from Phelan and swung the ball across the face of the goal, catching Jim Leighton once again in two minds and groping thin air. Ian Wright timed his run impeccably and launched himself into the air to punch the ball home with his right foot and put Palace 3-2 ahead. It was a simple goal, but brilliantly executed, and it felt for all the world like the winner until just seven minutes from the end, when Mark Hughes again levelled the scores. United had come back into it with their best football of the whole game, and always looked like scoring, but the goal when it came was a slightly soft one: O'Reilly's momentary lapse of concentration allowed Hughes into a scoring position from where he just managed to squeeze the ball agonisingly between the defender and the goalkeeper. The final score of 3-3 left the fans not knowing what to do with themselves, unable to celebrate or drown their sorrows, and knowing that they had to go through the whole exhausting process in a replay; after such an afternoon, the appropriate response was to sing: "We're proud of you".

RICHARD SHAW

Not too many people really wanted a replay, but of course Ron Noades was one who relished the prospect, Palace having a much bigger allocation of tickets to sell due to the absence from the second game of all the freeloaders and corporate shindiggers. Nevertheless, the arrangements for selling tickets were a complete shambles, with nobody having a clue what was going on even as the queues were forming on the Sunday morning. The most shameful profit-making enterprise is the club's telephone ticket information service, whereby you are made to pay an excessive amount to find out information which most other forms of entertainment provide via the box-office, or even on a free telephone number. Even this, at 25 pence a minute, was unforgivably giving out the wrong information all Sunday morning, but of course there is no mechanism for getting your money back. After all the hard luck stories from the first game, this time it appeared that everyone who wanted a ticket was able to get one, but the replay turned out to be a major let-down.

While nobody could honestly claim that Palace deserved to win, the same can certainly be said for Manchester United, and it was undeniably a bad game. The Palace players were heavily criticised for their physical approach to the match, but I sincerely believe that this was not a deliberate tactical ploy by Coppell, rather an ill-advised reaction by individual players to United's similar style in the first game. Players such as Wallace, Hughes and especially Robson, not only rely on systematic foul play as part of their game, but have the gall to appear outraged if they are penalised for it. Robson's reputation for intimidating referees into letting him get away with murder was a feature of his game for many years, but reached a peak as his effectiveness as a player diminished, yet he still retained his image as a world-class player despite scant supporting evidence. This ugly attitude to the game typified the United team throughout the 1989-90 season, but it was Palace who bore all the brickbats, having taken United on at their own game and lost. To my mind, Coppell's great error was in keeping Ian Wright back as substitute for the replay; the game was there to be won and a more positive approach by Palace may well have won the cup, but Coppell stuck to the tactics of containment and Palace never looked very dangerous up front, although they were denied a clear penalty. The winning goal was a good one: Neil Webb's found his left back Lee Martin in space, having got away from Andy Gray, and he hit the shot extremely well, but United should be no more proud of their performance than Palace, who actually had the more chances. Perhaps the decisive factor was Alex Ferguson's brave and difficult decision to drop his good friend Jim Leighton from the team, and bring in the on-loan goalkeeper Les Sealey, whose safe handling significantly settled the United defence.

It was a very sad night – not because Palace lost, but because they played badly – but already the memory of that game is fading fast. The images that will remain are those of the red and blue balloons and ribbons, the singing, the feeling of togetherness and – dare I say it – community, that are rarely experienced and which are almost becoming unique to the game of football, at least in this country. The semi-final victory over Liverpool and the drawn final were two of the greatest days ever, and what was important to the fans was not really the final outcome, but the fact that they were there, and part of it.

"WE'RE PROUD OF YOU"

Goalkeepers

No contest: **John Jackson** was without doubt the finest goalkeeper to play for Palace, and one of the best in the country. He was not only capable of making miraculous saves, but produced them week after week until one came to take them for granted. He saved so many certain goals that, without him, Palace would never have stayed in the First Division for as long as they did, and his loyalty to Palace

JOHN JACKSON

probably denied him the chance of playing for England, although he did turn out once for a representative Football League side. It was often said that if he had been born anywhere but England he would certainly have played for his country, but I would argue that only Gordon Banks was his superior, and that Jacko should have been his understudy in the England team. The worst decision that Malcolm Allison ever made was to sell Jackson to Orient in 1973, and I maintain that Palace would not have been relegated that season had he stayed in goal, instead of the younger and vastly inferior Paul Hammond. In his attitude to the game and his dedication he was the model professional, and the sort of player that any youngster should look up to and admire, and more than ever football needs more like him. There have been other goalkeepers, of course, and it is worth having a look at their claims, but as Jackson was my complete hero his is the

one place in this make-believe team that is sacred.

Paul Hammond had to bear the burden of Malcolm Allison's patronage in preference to Jackson, and after keeping goal after a fashion as Palace slid down through the Second Division spent the next three seasons alternating between the sticks with **Tony Burns**. Hammond was a competent technician when it came to positioning and handling of crosses, but rarely made saves out of the ordinary, while the more experienced Burns was at least a better shouter. After the blandness of these two, the contrast when **John Burridge** took over was enormous, and quite apart from his clowning he was also a very good player. Burridge was ever-present in the Second Division championship season of 1978-79, and his irrepressible enthusiasm had a positive influence on the young defenders in front of him. However much he enjoyed entertaining the crowd, he was fanatical about perfecting his own game, and any goal that went past him made him furious, unable to accept that some goals just can't be helped. The circumstances of Burridge's departure were symptomatic of the chronic malaise running through the club after 1979, and although he didn't actually leave until following Venables to QPR, he had fallen out over his contract long before that, and was replaced in the team by **Paul Barron**, from Arsenal. Barron was by no means as bad as his reputation nowadays would have one believe, but he had the bad luck to play for Palace during one of their worst ever periods, and he could have been Dino Zoff for all the difference it would have made.

After Alan Mullery had sold Barron to West Bromwich Albion, **David Fry** played out the rest of the 1982-83 season, but Mullery then went out and bought another Arsenal reserve, the bird-watching Scotsman **George Wood**, who only missed three games in the next five years before his ignominious end in 1988.

Wood was never the quickest of players, but he was better than his immediate predecessors, and played consistently well until quite near the end. In his final season he was increasingly being blamed for a number of goals, particularly away from home, but the final straw for Steve Coppell was the disastrous 4-4 result at Leicester, Wood shouldering the blame for throwing away three points. After Wood had conceded 13 goals in five games, Coppell took decisive action and bought the England Under-21 keeper **Perry Suckling** from Manchester City, with Wood going to Cardiff. Suckling was quicker, sharper, more agile, and above all younger than Wood, and being a local boy the fans took to him at once. He had trouble with his kicking leg which meant him missing most of the first half of the 1988-89 season, and although **Brian Parkin** did a good job in his place, Suckling's return coincided with a run of good form that ultimately lifted Palace towards the play-offs. Suckling played a heroic part in winning promotion, and it was hard luck on such a likeable character that he should become the butt of so many cruel jokes after Liverpool's 9-0 win the following season. It is to his credit that after Palace had spent £1 million on Nigel Martyn to replace him, Suckling didn't indulge in any petulant outbursts, but instead got on with trying to play his way back into form, and did a particularly good job by all accounts when on loan to West Ham. Let's hope that he gets the chance before too long to re-establish himself with a decent club.

Nigel Martyn came to Palace having already been spoken of as a future England goalkeeper, and I find it hard to understand why anyone should complain at the amount spent on him, since to my mind a really good goalkeeper is one of the most valuable assets a team can have. Martyn's first season for Palace was inconclusive, and there were several goals conceded for which he was certainly at fault, but even in that short time one could see that he had a special quality about him that might one day make him a great player, and the way he handled himself during the F.A.Cup semi-final and final was truly impressive. Whether he makes the progress needed to establish himself in the England team will depend a lot on how Palace's defence shape up in front of him, but my guess – rather my hope – is that we will soon hail Nigel Martyn as "the new John Jackson", and I can think of no higher compliment.

Full Backs

One player stands out from all the others as an automatic selection for the left back position. **Kenny Sansom** was the best of the impressively talented youth team who won the F.A. Youth Cup for two years running, most of whom graduated to the first team, and the First Division. Playing in a side which concentrated on accurate passing and building patiently from the back, Sansom was the starting point for many of Palace's attacking moves. The basis of his game was his usually faultless first time control, which meant that each tackle or interception he made was not simply defensive, but also gained constructive possession of the ball. Uniquely for a Palace

KENNY SANSOM

defender he was able to take the ball past opposing players and make space for himself, and at times he was hardly seen as a defender, because he was so often in attacking mode. Before he had established himself in the first team, he learnt an early disciplinary lesson when being suspended after using "industrial language" in a youth game, but thereafter he had the good sense to keep his temper, confident in the knowledge that he was undoubtedly a superior footballer. His first full season came after Venables had taken over as manager from Malcolm Allison, a season which ended with promotion to the Second Division thanks largely to an excellent

defence. Over the next two years his form helped Palace climb back into Division One, and also made him an obvious contender for a place in the England team, where he became a fixture over the next nine years. After the "team of the eighties" bubble had burst, his move to Arsenal – in exchange for Clive Allen – signalled the beginning of a rapid decline for Palace. The conventional wisdom is that Sansom needed his cut of the transfer fee to get himself out of a financial hole, being a notorious gambler, but as usual the fans were kept in the dark about the deteriorating atmosphere behind the scenes, which temporarily wrecked the club.

It is true to say that there are few genuine contenders for the left back position in this imaginary team, and the list of those who have filled that shirt is rather uninspiring, including as it does such functional players as **John Loughlan**, **Bill Roffey**, **Les Strong** and **Brian Sparrow**. **Stewart Jump** wasn't a bad player at all, but he seemed to be playing in the wrong position somehow, and Terry Fenwick was never a defender, although incredibly he went on to play as a centre back for England later in his career. **Paul Brush** played his part in Palace's revival under Steve Coppell before he submitted to recurrent injuries, and his successor **David Burke**, despite being prone to frequent errors of an elementary nature, was at least a true left back, and contributed to some valuable goals when swinging crosses over from that side in the promotion year of 1988-89.

Early in the career of **Mark Dennis**, he was considered one of England's brightest young hopes, but he repeatedly ruined his chances with his violent temperament, and the great shame is that in the few games he played for Palace between injuries in 1989-90, he impressed the sceptical supporters as potentially an extremely good player indeed. It is too early to say yet whether left back will be **Richard Shaw**'s best position as he progresses, but his performances against Aston Villa's Tony Daley, and Peter Beardsley in the F.A.Cup semi final against Liverpool were outstanding in their own right, and he could turn out to be a very fine player, although perhaps more naturally at right back.

Apart from Jim Cannon, who I will deal with as a centre back although he played for two years in the No.3 shirt, the only other player worthy of consideration in this position is **Peter Wall**, who was with the club for eight years, although he broke his leg twice in that time, and missed long periods as a consequence. I always got the impression that Wall had more ability than he ever bothered to use, and that he sometimes felt that he should actually still be playing for his previous

PETER WALL

employers, Liverpool. Bought as a left back by Bert Head, by the time Malcolm Allison had taken over at Palace, a serious break sustained against Liverpool meant that Wall had been effectively replaced, first of all by Tony Taylor, and then by Stewart Jump and Jim Cannon. Although he made a brief comeback in 1973-74, the season when Palace slid straight down through Division 2, he was then out of action again until the latter part of the following season, when he replaced Paddy Mulligan as right back, and stayed there during

the famous cup run of 1976. Although naturally left footed, he appeared just as confident on the right, and even played a few games as a kind of sweeper, a job which would have suited him very well if he had been a bit quicker. He eventually left the club in 1977, to play in the North American Soccer League, where his languid and intelligent style would, I am sure, have been well appreciated.

Whilst I cannot place Peter Wall ahead of Sansom for the left back position, then, I would certainly make a case for him at right back, another position where Palace haven't been terribly successful over the past 20 years, with **Brian Bason**, **Gary Locke**, **Gary Stebbing** and **Steve Lovell** being among those who I wouldn't want to consider for too long. In fact, Steve Lovell became an extremely prolific goalscorer after leaving Palace, at a time when Alan Mullery was desperate for a decent forward, and he must have been cursing his lack of judgement, which the supporters did from the day he came to the club.

A player who made the opposite transition, from striker to right back, was the curious looking **Paul Hinshelwood**, whose puny frame and curly hair earned him the nickname, derogatory at first, but ultimately affectionate, of 'Doris'. Hinshelwood was a fixture in the team that won the Second Division title in 1979, and as promotion was built on a remarkably good defensive record, he must take his share of the credit along with his colleagues, Sansom, Cannon and Billy Gilbert. His main strength, though, was in going forward, and although he didn't score too often, occasionally the ball would fall nicely into his stride as he galloped towards goal, and he would let fly with a fierce shot. Just like Sansom on the left, Hinshelwood was the starting point for a good deal of Palace's attacking manoeuvres, having received the ball from Burridge, but he did not have Sansom's talent for close control, so the longer ball up the touchline was more usual on that side of the field. What endeared Doris to the fans was not his playing ability, but his dogged determination to overcome his failings as a defender. Faced by a fast and skilful winger, he would crouch a few yards off his man all the way down the touchline, staring intently at the ball, until he was shown just enough of it to attempt the tackle. The lunge, when it came, ' would more often than not miss the ball and connect with the legs, but his fouls were always of a clumsy, even comical nature, rather than what you would call dirty. The vogue for Crystal Palace players at one time even earned Hinshelwood two England Under-21 caps, but effective though he was when things were going well, he was never more than an ordinary, if eccentric player, and after staying through the upheavals of the early 1980's, he was sold by Mullery to Oxford, and replaced by Gary Locke.

All of Palace's right backs from then on until the arrival of **John Pemberton** were being used in that position as a makeshift measure, and arguably the best of them was **Tony Finnigan**, really an attacking midfield player who was sold prematurely to Blackburn, and who could have done a better job in midfield than either Pennyfather or Pardew. **Gary Stebbing** was a player who never looked comfortable whatever position he played in, although he had shown promise as a youth – even playing for England – and he was always the target of abuse from a frustrated crowd, which left him without any confidence at all. **Henry Hughton** was another player more at home in midfield, and never the equal of his more famous brother, and the jury is still out on the latest incumbent, Pemberton, who deserved more praise than he got, despite occasional outrageous errors.

Looking further back, of course **John Sewell** must be considered strongly, more for his qualities as a captain than for anything else. With his upright bearing and his always immaculate appearance, he appeared to belong to another era even at the time of his greatest success, leading Palace to the First Division for the first time ever in 1969. Unusually, perhaps uniquely for a team skipper, Sewell made a point of never arguing with the referee, and took pride in the fact that he had never been booked. Most of his few goals came from the penalty spot, but his aimless punt against Gary Sprake in his final season with Palace, 1970-71, was one of the most memorable goals ever scored at Selhurst Park, and ensures his place for ever in Palace folklore. Sewell's successor, **David Payne**, did a fair job after being converted from midfield, but was always the ultimate utility player, and **Paddy Mulligan**, the Irish International, was injured so often that he rarely strung more than half a dozen games together. Mulligan's greatest moment at Palace was when he scored two of the five goals against Manchester United in 1972, the only time he scored for the club.

To summarise, then, with Sansom an obvious choice for left back, the other full back spot rests between John Sewell, Paul Hinshelwood and Peter Wall, with the last named being the selection simply because, even though he was more naturally a left sided player, on his best form he looked like a First Division player taking it easy, rather than a Second Division player struggling to keep up.

Centre Backs

If a player is described as 'craggy', the chances are that he's a tall, red-headed Scottish centre half, and **John McCormick** was a perfect example of the species. Big Mac was ever present in the 1968-69 promotion side, along with Jackson and Kember, and kept his place until being dropped to accommodate Bobby Bell in 1973, at the age of 36. Although physically very tough, he was by no means a

JOHN McCORMICK

dirty player, and set an example to his colleagues with his supreme application to the job. When heading a ball either in defence or attack he seemed to use every muscle in his body for maximum power, and was the last player ever to let his head drop if things were going badly. No one would claim that he was the most skilful of players in possession, but his timing in the tackle was always accurate and efficient, and his positional sense compensated for the occasional waywardness of his partner, Mel Blyth. As a traditional 'stopper' he was one of the best, and would have deserved a place in any Palace side since.

Mel Blyth was in fact deposed as centre back for a while by yet another Scotsman, **Roger Hynd,** but after playing in midfield for much of the 1969-70 season he won his place back when Hynd was temporarily switched to the forward line. Blyth liked to play his way out of

defence, but the execution didn't always match the ambition, and he often found himself getting into trouble. Nevertheless, the contrasting styles of Blyth and McCormick made for a good mix, and the two of them stayed together until McCormick's retirement, near the end of Bert Head's time in charge. Blyth continued on and off throughout Malcolm Allison's first, disastrous year, before being sold cheaply to Southampton in the same week that Ian Evans arrived from QPR. His move to The Dell renewed his enthusiasm and there he played the best football of his career as a member of the side that beat Palace in the F.A.Cup semi-final, going on to collect a winners' medal. Two years later he came back to Selhurst Park on loan, ironically to fill the gap left after Ian Evans' awful injury, before giving way to the next No.6, Billy Gilbert. Blyth's reputation was completely the opposite of John McCormick's, both on the field and off it, and he was always likely to get into trouble with referees, once being sent off in a game against Everton for elbowing the niggling Alan Whittle, then playing for the Toffeemen. After a newspaper had run an article about his playboy image, quoting him as saying "..my Saturday night ends late on Sunday morning - it's devoted exclusively to birds and booze", he was given the programme space normally devoted to Bert Head's utterances to put the record straight, and he expressed his disgust that the article had "made me out to be some kind of raver", although it certainly had the ring of truth. Blyth's fellow central defenders after McCormick were a fairly motley bunch, with Allison's supposed star of the future **Derek Jeffries** being the best and **Bobby Bell** probably the worst, with the hard man **Roy Barry** somewhere in between, but when **Ian Evans** succeeded Blyth, Palace at last had a really good central defender in the team.

Evans came as part of the package with Terry Venables, and it was a bold move for a player with such an obviously bright future to drop down to the Third Division, but we were glad that he did. For the next three years Evans was the key player in a Palace team that, although unable to climb out of Division Three, played good, entertaining football to big crowds, and surprised everyone by reaching the last four of the F.A.Cup, which was no fluke. Initially partnered by Derek Jeffries, with Jim Cannon at left back, Evans was clearly a player of great ability, but once Cannon joined him in

IAN EVANS

the centre he looked superb. Both players were ever-present, together with Kenny Sansom, in Terry Venables' first season as manager, when Palace finally made it back to the Second Division, and they looked set to go straight up to the First the following year, until Evans broke his leg against Fulham, in a tackle with George Best. Evans' recovery was painfully slow, and by the time he was fit again, Billy Gilbert had established himself in the side, and Evans finished his playing days at Barnsley, before coming back to Palace in 1984 as Steve Coppell's assistant.

Jim Cannon had made an impact in his first ever game for Palace, when he scored the second goal in the victory against Chelsea that signalled Allison's arrival, but it took him a couple of years, playing mainly at left back, to establish himself in the first team. He really

matured when he played alongside Evans, and by the time Billy Gibert came into the side Cannon was one of the team's senior players, at the age of 24. In nearly 15 years of service, under a total of seven managers, Cannon was often the one player who could be relied on perform consistently well, and after a while it was difficult to imagine Crystal Palace without him, his 568 league appearances giving him a club record that is unlikely to be beaten. Although he was often touted as a potential Scottish International, he was probably just short of that level, but as a club player he was the type that is invaluable. When he was feeling confident he would set off on a gallop that took him into a shooting position, which was only occasionally successful, but most of his few goals came from headers, and he was always a danger at the far post from corners. His best remembered goal, though, was the fourth against Ipswich in 1979 that sent Palace to the top of Division One, the day that both he and his team were at their peak.

Cannon's regular partner for some seven years was **Billy Gilbert**, a straightforward player with few frills, although like everyone else in Venables' team of 1979 he had the confidence early in his career to play a quality of football that later gave way to a more basic defensive strategy, depending rather more on intimidation. Gilbert had long spells of very good form with interludes when nothing would go right, but his final season at Palace was his best for a long time and I for one was sorry to see him go to Portsmouth, although things were in such a state under Alan Mullery that one could hardly blame him for wanting to get away. When Coppell took charge, then, one of his many problems was finding a replacement for Billy Gilbert – although **John Lacy** was on the staff, he wisely looked elsewhere - and after **Chris Whyte**'s too brief sojourn, and experiments with Gavin Nebbeling and Gary Stebbing, he persuaded Chelsea's Titan **Micky Droy** to form a formidable team with Jim Cannon. Although this was only a short term solution, the difference that Droy made to the defence was a major factor in Palace's revival the following year, and it was typically shrewd of Coppell to give him the job, at the age of 34.

After Droy had finally slowed to a halt, **Gavin Nebbeling** showed significant improvement in his game to win back his place, but was soon under threat from the former Spurs and Brighton player **Gary O'Reilly**, and these two vied for the No.5 shirt for the next three seasons, although O'Reilly missed a lot of that time through injury. Both players were very strong in the air, but less sure of themselves on the ground, although to my mind O'Reilly was certainly the better player, as well as coming over as a thoroughly nice character from his intelligent and articulate appearances on the radio. All this time Jim Cannon had been the one constant factor in a changing defence, but after coming close to promotion for three years running, Coppell decided that his skipper had served his purpose, and shocked some of his admirers by giving him a free transfer.

Jeff Hopkins was the player bought to replace Cannon, and he has yet to win the fans over despite playing a big part in Palace's promotion to Division One. When at his best he looks a perfectly good player, but his confidence too often seems to desert him and he is sometimes guilty of disastrous lapses of concentration, like his own goals against Swindon in the play-offs and Millwall in the First Division. After the 9-0 Nightmare at Anfield, a priority was obviously to spend some money on a centre half with some authority, and following protracted negotiation Palace landed **Andy Thorn**, one of Wimbledon's Cup-winning team who had used that opportunity to get away from Plough Lane, ending up at Newcastle. The prosaic reputation of that side worried those who hadn't seen Thorn play, but he quickly proved himself to be an excellent bargain, a player around whom an entire defence can be structured. Once he came into

the side Palace always appeared likely to stay in Division One, and he acted as a talisman all the way to Wembley, raising the game of those around him, particularly Gary O'Reilly in the Cup semi-final and final.

Thorn may yet be one of the best central defenders Palace have had, but for my team the player who holds that title, quite comfortably, is Ian Evans, despite his career being cut short by such a bad injury. I think Jim Cannon would earn a place in most fans' imaginary sides, and it is difficult to argue against his selection, but sentiment steers me towards John McCormick – one of my first idols – whose image always comes to mind when I think of the old claret and blue colours.

Midfielders

The main feature of Bert Head's successful team was a willingness to graft for each other, and while players like **David Payne** and **Roger Hoy** had this quality in abundance, the only outfield player who made his mark as an outstanding individual was the young midfielder from Croydon, **Steve Kember**. Although he was still only 20 years old in the promotion year of 1969, he had been a first team regular for over three years and there had never been any doubt that he was bound for the First Division, be it with Palace or with a larger club. He had everything you could ask for in a midfield player, being both a tenacious ball winner and always intelligent and adventurous with his distribution, and the Palace team was built around his skills for the five years leading up to his sudden departure in 1971, when he was sold to Chelsea for a record fee of £170,000. This was a great shock for the team and the fans, but the truth was that since going up they had failed to make progress, and Kember had little choice but to leave if he was to stand a chance of pressing his claims for a place in the England team. The great shame was that he joined a Chelsea side in serious decline, and never made it beyond the national Under-23 team, because in the right environment he could have become one of the great players of the Seventies.

After rather fading into obscurity with Leicester, he answered Terry Venables' call to rejoin his old club in 1978, and his experience and devotion to the cause was the single most important factor in Palace's successful push for promotion, although the kudos went mostly to the precocious youngsters, several of whom had benefitted years earlier from Kember's laudable interest in coaching juniors in his own time. It was no surprise that Kember was the fans' choice as manager after Dario Gradi was sacked in 1981, but he was given a pitifully short time in which to prove himself, being sacked after six months and replaced by Mullery. I am sure I am not alone in thinking that someone who had done so much for Palace,

and who still has such an affinity with the supporters, deserved better treatment, although Kember's innate dignity prevents him from expressing any grudge against the club.

There has been nobody since who I would

STEVE KEMBER

consider so adept as Kember in every department, although there have been several midfielders to admire for their own particular qualities. Kember's successor in 1971 – who had also been his predecessor until 1965 – was **Bobby Kellard**; energetic, equally dogged, and also a big favourite with the fans, but without the creative imagination that was so needed in that struggling side. Kellard in turn was superseded by two Scotsmen who were very disappointing in their different ways; **Charlie Cooke** had been a great player, but had little left to give Palace, while **Iain Philip** – at the time Palace's most expensive signing, at £115,000 – was a star of the future who came to nothing, lasting just a year before returning to Dundee.

Allison's first, woeful season in charge was characterised by indecision concerning selection that saw several inappropriate players used in midfield, including Mel Blyth, Jim Cannon, Derek Jeffries and Don Rogers, with only **Jeff Johnson** and **Mark Lindsay** looking vaguely at home. After **Terry Venables** had padded round for a few games, Allison's best period came when **Nicky Chatterton** combined with **Martin Hinshelwood** and **Phil Holder** in midfield, a solid, hard working unit which nearly took Palace to Wembley, and should have won promotion in 1976. Holder, formerly with Spurs, was a pugnacious little footballer in the mould of Bobby Kellard, while Hinshelwood was infinitely more elegant, although desperately fragile. Chatterton was somewhere between the two of them, and although he also had frequent interruptions through injury, he was a fixture in Palace's team for five years, until finally being replaced by Kember in 1978, and moving to Millwall. Chatterton was typical of the kind of 'worker' that most good teams contain, very much a team player like David Payne or, latterly, Alan Pardew, who also scored his share of goals each season, and who managed to win most genuine fans over, despite being the 'boo-boy' for a while. For a couple of seasons Chatterton was required to do the running around on behalf of **George Graham**, known as 'Stroller', and never was a nickname more apt. Graham had been a member of Arsenal's double-winning side, and had once scored the winning 'Goal of the Season' on The Big Match, against Palace. He was undoubtedly a skilful player in possession of the ball, slowing the play down and opening up obscure avenues of attack, but he seemed to miss nearly as many games through suspension as through injury, and his cynicism as a player has since found expression through the teams he has gone on to manage.

The most successful midfield combination of the Seventies was the one that formed the core of Terry Venables' Second Division Championship winners of 1979, comprising Kember, Peter Nicholas and Jerry Murphy, with the occasional contribution from Terry Fenwick. **Peter Nicholas** first came into the side as a makeshift defender, but once moved to the right of midfield it soon became obvious

that he was set to become one of the game's natural captains; hard in the tackle and strong going forward, from early on he was spoken of as the heir to Terry Yorath's Welsh crown. His contemporary, **Jerry Murphy**, couldn't have been more different, and relied on the endeavours of Kember and Nicholas to allow him to practice his ambitious, audacious and often sublime skills. Murphy loved to show what he could do by delicately chipping the ball with backspin wherever possible, but although everyone knew what a good player he was, he ultimately let himself down because he wasn't able to graft in the same way as someone like Nicholas and consequently became stuck in a very deep rut at Palace, finally being the last of Venables' great team to leave in 1985, Jim Cannon excepted.

When Palace went up in 1979, Venables' most important addition to the side was **Gerry Francis**, an exceptional player at one time with QPR, but by now significantly slower than he needed to be, although he was superb in midfield in that wonderful first half of the season, and still showed glimpses of genius. After everything collapsed the following year, Francis followed Venables back to Loftus Road, leaving the midfield in the hands of such players as the would-be boy wonder **Shaun Brooks**, the portly **David Price**, and a variety of uninspiring characters like **Steve Lovell**, **Gary Stebbing** and **Henry Hughton**. **Steve Galliers** offered little more than manic effort and a frightening tackle, but matters only really improved when another former Wimbledon man, **Steve Ketteridge**, linked up with **Kevin Taylor**, and Palace finally started winning again in 1985. Ketteridge in particular would chase everything, and Taylor could play a bit of football, and with these two solid in the middle Coppell was able to build a simple, effective structure that has evolved along the same lines ever since. Where Ketteridge was weakest was in going forward, and he was replaced by **Andy Gray**, by instinct a striker, but who looked a natural once switched to a creative midfield role. Gray's successful conversion meant that, with himself and Taylor both exclusively right-sided, Palace were on the look out for a new left-footer, and the man plucked by Steve Coppell from the obscurity of Crewe Alexandra – **Geoff Thomas** – was to prove one of his shrewdest buys. With Gray throwing himself all over the place and being generally flash, Thomas applied himself to the task of holding everything together in the middle, fiercely protective of the ball once in possession and organising those around him, which led to him becoming the obvious choice as captain after Jim Cannon had gone.

GEOFF THOMAS

Thomas was an outstanding success in his first season, but was forced to miss the second half of the 1988-89 promotion season with an injury, which left the midfield places to be fought out by **Super Alan Pardew**, **Glenn Pennyfather** and, most impressively, **Dave Madden**. Pardew's sturdy contribution was to grow in importance throughout the year, although he was never as powerful as Thomas, but as a creative force Dave Madden was the key player, often showing skills far beyond what one would have expected from a reject from Reading. Madden lost his place the following season after the return of the prodigal

son, Andy Gray, but when Thomas was forced to play in defence his place went instead to Pardew, who held on to it all season. Madden finally got a look in only at the very end of the season, and came on as a substitute in the two Wembley finals before leaving on a free transfer, for what reason we have yet to discover.

As the 1989-90 season wore on, with Gray forced to play wide on the right wing, Geoff Thomas gradually began to come back to his best form, and showed some of his nicest touches in the Cup games, including a cracking equaliser against Portsmouth and some assured and incisive passing against Liverpool and Manchester United. In the expectation that Thomas will add to his already considerable talents with another year's experience in Division One, I have no hesitation in selecting him for my team together with Steve Kember, although I am bound to say that Jerry Murphy was always a favourite of mine, and if I was able to select only his best moments he would be a major contender.

Wingers

It is very difficult to discuss the relative merits of various Palace wingers since the term itself can be misleading, and I am using it here to embrace the whole range of wide attacking players, few of whom would have been regarded as true wingers in Stanley Matthews' day. If one was to be pedantic, then clearly players like Jim Scott, Bobby Tambling and John Craven could not be called wingers in the way that Neil Smillie or Alan Irvine could, but essentially their function was the same. Indeed, some people would claim that Steve Coppell himself was a wide midfielder for England rather than a winger, but the distinction is too fine to be concerned with.

Palace won promotion in 1969 using two wingers who also happened to be better than average goalscorers; **Mark Lazarus** on the right and **Colin Taylor** on the left. Both were stocky little players who looked about ten years older than they were, and Taylor in particular had an awsomely powerful shot when the goal was in his sights, scoring the winning goal in the famous 2-1 victory over mighty Leeds United in the League Cup. However, Taylor soon returned to Walsall, and Lazarus only played a handful of First Division games before moving on to Orient, leaving the fitness fanatic **Tony Taylor** as the only wide player until **Jimmy Scott** and **Bobby Tambling** arrived the following year.

Scott had the knack of dribbling past two or three defenders before falling over the ball or running straight into touch, and only managed a few goals in his short time at Palace, but the former England International Bobby Tambling was Palace's top league scorer during the 1971-72 season, albeit with only eight goals. His best goal for Palace was in the Anglo-Italian Tournament, against Luigi Riva's Cagliari side, when he somehow found the net with a swinging left foot shot from almost the corner flag, although some observers put it down as a fluke. Another previously prolific scorer whose goals dried up when he moved to Palace was

the ex-Bolton winger **Terry Wharton**, and following him came **John Craven**, strong and direct and often the only player in the team who looked like he wanted to go forward, although it was sometimes difficult to fathom where Bert Head wanted him to play.

At the same time as Craven arrived came **John 'Yogi Bear' Hughes** into the outside left position, and although he scored one of the great Palace goals of all time, against Sheffield United, he did little else between injuries before being sold to Sunderland, and was replaced by **Don Rogers**. At last Palace had bought a star name, if only from the Third Division, and Rogers was an instant success at Selhurst Park, scoring a goal in his debut that was a prototype for many others to come, although he played for less than two full seasons. His great assett was a burst of speed

DON ROGERS

from a standing position that made a mug out of more than one apparently quick defender, and any ball played through for him to chase brought the crowd to their feet in anticipation of another spectacular solo run, finished off by rounding the keeper or arrogantly chipping the ball over his prostrate body. Having found himself with one of the First Division's most exciting and effective wingers, Malcolm Allison then hatched a cunning plan, master tactician that he was, which effectively converted Rogers into a central midfielder, and he was never the same exhilarating player again. It certainly wasn't that Allison had any great ideological objection to wingers, because he soon went out and bought a player with a similar style, right down to the crouch; **Peter Taylor** from Southend.

Despite his brilliance, Taylor couldn't save Palace from dropping to Division Three, but he did all he could to drag them back up again, in the process earning himself rave notices and a call up for his country, and inspiring the 1976 F.A.Cup run to the semi-final. After two seasons stuck in the Third Division the lure of Spurs was too great for Taylor to resist, but Terry Venables, in his first season as Palace manager, finally won promotion using either **Rachid Harkouk** or **Barry Silkman** on the left, and these two alternated for a couple of seasons until the prodigious talent of **Vince Hilaire** forced him into the team, initially as a centre forward, but then more usefully on the

VINCE HILAIRE

left wing. Hilaire was handicapped early on by the high expectations of him created by Allison's ravings and his own documentary on T.V., but he turned out to be every bit as good as hyped, and when forging links with Sansom and Murphy along the left touchline he was capable of the most extraordinary

flashes of genius, with wonderful control and an uncanny ability to breeze past full-backs, although the final cross was too often found wanting. The other criticism was that he was reluctant to have a go at goal himself, having torn the defence to shreds, but his real problem – strangely, for one so gifted – was a lack of confidence.

During the dark years of the early Eighties, **Neil Smillie** and **David Giles** were the two other winger used by Dario Gradi, Steve Kember and Alan Mullery, but as the team crumbled around him Hilaire was for long periods the only good reason for going to watch Palace, and he finally left before Coppell arrived, probably having stayed loyal too long for his own good. If Palace had been successful in that period then Hilaire would surely have been in the running for England honours, but his career had gone steadily off course, and he was sadly never able to become the star that he should have been, although he continued to play brilliantly in patches.

Coppell's first winger, **Alan Irvine**, was extremely basic, very effective going forward down the right hand touchline and getting crosses in to the centre, but strictly limited to this function. The use of such a straightforward ploy was clearly to Coppell's liking, though, and Irvine was followed by **Neil Redfearn**, who added an element of defensive strength to the position that Irvine had lacked, and who was more willing to take up positions other than out wide, which rendered him more useful to the midfield as a whole.

Meanwhile, two very different players were vying for the left wing position, but it was eventually **Phil Barber** who was to become the manager's choice ahead of the more gifted **John Salako**. The fact that Barber is always referred to as 'Mr. 110%' betrays the fact that his effort and dedication far outstrip his ability, but those are qualities not to be sneered at. Having come to Palace from Aylesbury originally as a striker, Barber was the only survivor from Alan Mullery's squad to make it to the First Division with Palace, and his propensity for hard work obviously impressed Steve Coppell, who used him in a number of positions before he finally settled wide on the left, although you wouldn't call him a winger in the strictest sense since he was never blessed with great speed. Despite enduring years of scorn and abuse from the fans – and I have always been one of his many critics – it was heartening to see Barber play his part in Palace's Cup run; scoring against Rochdale, setting up goals for Bright against Huddersfield and for Thomas at Cambridge and playing a tight marking game, almost as a left back, in the semi-final and final. He took the free kick that led to the first goal at Wembley, and to eventually come away with only a loser's medal after coming so far must have been especially distressing for Barber, knowing that he was unlikely to play there again in his life.

In contrast to Barber, the born-again Christian John Salako at his best is fast, skilful and exciting, but he suffers from the old wingers' syndrome of disappearing from the game for long periods and is not yet strong enough to fight to win possession, although he did a superb job in the Cup games, marking closely, tackling accurately and running his legs off. At Wembley he showed something of his ability as a forward with his control and cross for Ian Wright's second goal, and I sincerely hope that that experience will make him resolve to fight for his place in the team, because it would be a terrible shame for Palace to lose such a popular player.

The final winger under consideration is the man who took over from Redfearn after **Alex Dyer** had played a handful of games; another of Steve Coppell's finds from the lower divisions, the former Northampton player **Eddie McGoldrick**. With his moustache and surprised look, Eddie cuts a comical figure, and played an important part in promotion, but as yet he hasn't looked at home in the First Division, and it is unlikely that he will ever rank alongside the two players chosen for this team, Don Rogers and Vince Hilaire, with Peter Taylor a very close third.

Strikers

There have been two distinct species of striker in the modern game, and British football at least has been loathe to look for alternatives. The first is the 'Big No. 9', tall, strong, good with his head and happy to take 90 minutes of hard knocks. The second type, evolved from the inside-forward of old, is lighter, quicker, usually more skilful and looking to profit from the knock-down or touch-off from his partner. This combination has been evident at most successful clubs and some classic examples from the past are Chivers and Gilzean at Spurs, and Jones and Clarke at Leeds. Strangely, the English national team has had precious little success using this system, and of late have relied up front on Lineker and Beardsley, reluctant to repeat the mistake made with Mark Hateley. At Palace, easily their most successful attacking partnership – that of Mark Bright and Ian Wright – is a perfect example of the system at its best, but there have been a few others to consider over the years, and I shall start by looking at the 'target men', of which there haven't been too many.

Palace's centre-forward in Bert Head's promotion side of 1969 was **Bobby Woodruff**, a consistent scorer with good timing in the air and a notable long throw, but too gentle a soul to make his mark after helping the team into Division One. After Woodruff had left, only having played a few games in the First Division, there was a gap until **Alan Birchenall** arrived the following season, as Palace's first £100,000 signing. Birchenall never looked as good as he was supposed to be, and although he always worked hard he spent most of the time with his back to the goal, knocking the ball down to nobody in particular, and was rarely in positions to score himself. Maybe he would have had more luck in a better side, but Chelsea didn't seem to miss him too much, although he epitomised their lingering 'swinging sixties' image, claiming that he used to sing with Joe Cocker in Sheffield.

Following Birchenall were a succession of tiny forwards including Willie Wallace and Derek Possee, although the long, thin **Ross Jenkins** earned the distiction of probably being Palace's tallest player ever after progressing from the reserves to the first team for a few games. Perhaps Palace gave up on him too hastily, feeling that he was far too easy to knock off the ball, because when he re-emerged a few years later as the linchpin of Watford's spectacularly successful airborne attack force, he had changed into a strong, aggressive and effective player.

Another graduate from the youth team, **Dave Swindlehurst**, was given an early chance by Malcolm Allison, and after a slow start improved steadily to become Palace's highest scorer in recent years, with a total of 81 goals. Swindlehurst's big asset was his all-round physical strength, and it was this rather than any agility that won him a lot of balls in the

DAVE SWINDLEHURST

air, a good proportion of his goals coming from powerful headers, although he loved to try a spectacular volley from time to time. He once scored eight goals in a spell of nine games in 1975, and although he only scored one hat-trick – in the last game of 1977-78 – he was the only player who could guarantee a steady stream of goals throughout the season. He particularly benefitted from the service given by Peter Taylor on the wing, and his best season was when Palace reached the F.A.Cup semi-final in 1976, Swindlehurst scoring the winning goal in perhaps the greatest victory of that run, at Leeds United. He invariably scored in the key games, including one of the four against Wrexham that hauled Palace out of the Third Division in 1977, and a goal in each of the last three games of 1978-79, victories that won Palace the Second Division Championship. His partnership with Ian Walsh that year had been quite productive, but once in the First Division Venables decided to pair Swindlehurst with Mike Flanagan, which never really came off at all. Having spent so much money on Flanagan, Venables could hardly drop him, so it was Swindlehurst who paid the price, eventually being sold to Derby County. How Palace could have done with him in the years to come, and it wasn't until we he had been made to suffer such poor substitutes as **Tommy Langley**, **Ian Edwards** and **Chris Jones** that we really appreciated Swindlehurst's qualities, and yearned to have him back.

I suppose some people would regard **Clive Allen** as a classic English centre-forward, and there have certainly been enough clubs willing to employ him as such over the years, but quite frankly all we saw during his time at Palace were glimpses of hints of a suggestion of his 'potential', his greatness remaining well hidden.

Andy McCulloch was another of Alan Mullery's unsuccessful strikers, and at least his successor – **Trevor Aylott** – almost reached double figures in 1984-85, his nine goals comparing favourably to the seven collected by the top scorer the year before, **Tony Evans**. After Aylott's drawn out demise, both Andy Gray and Phil Barber had a go in the No. 9 shirt, but Steve Coppell finally struck gold when he bought **Mark Bright** from Leicester City, for only £75,000. Bright had been in the shadow of Gary Lineker and Alan Smith at

Leicester, and hadn't done himself justice when he finally got his chance in the first team, But Coppell saw something in him that others had missed, a keen intelligence in front of goal that more than made up for any deficiencies of speed or sharpness. Bright scored in his first game for Palace, a 3-3 draw with Ipswich, and spent the rest of the 1986-87 season fine tuning his partnership with Ian Wright, which produced spectacular results the following year when his 24 league goals made him Palace's highest scorer in a single season since the days of Johnny Byrne. He is a target man in the truest sense, with long clearances from goal invariably aimed towards his handsome head, and he has rarely been bested over the course of a game by any central defender. The fact that he demands such close attention in turn creates more space for his colleagues, but as well as setting up a good number of chances with little flicks of the head, and by holding the ball up to lay it off into somebody's stride, he has proved beyond doubt a precious instinct for scoring.

Perhaps the weakest part of his game is when it comes to long-range shots, but put the ball across the face of goal and Bright will be there to force it home with some part of his body, his face animated with a delight that signifies him as someone who loves the game as much as the fans themselves. In contrast to a lot of big forwards, who often tend to have a violent edge to their game, Bright is a gentleman even when he goes in hard, and it was completely uncharacteristic for him to stamp on a Sheffield Wednesday defender in 1989-90, for which he was deservedly sent off. Critics of Bright insist that he has only done so well thanks to being paired with Ian Wright, but I would say that the benefit has been entirely mutual, and that although Bright certainly isn't as fast or as skilful as his partner, his other qualities make him one of the very best of his type in the English game at the moment. Without doubt, Mark Bright's most memorable and spectacular goal was his unstoppable volley against Liverpool in the F.A.Cup semi-final, but he has won many a lesser game with more mundane goals, and I look forward to his second season in Division One with great anticipation.

While there are few of the 'Big No. 9's' to choose from – and we do not yet know enough about **Garry 'Rambo" Thompson** to make a judgement – the other type of forward, the scavenger, has been better represented at Palace, from the sideburned Cliff Jackson all the way up to Ian Wright. **Cliff Jackson** was originally a winger, and when he converted to centre-forward it was his speed on the ground above all else that made him dangerous, happy to let Woodruff get on with the job of challenging for the ball in the air. His best season was the promotion year of 1969, and he it was who scored the vital equaliser against Fulham after Palace had been 2-0 down, which he celebrated with his renowned 'gladiator' salute. He had a less happy time in the First Division, largely due to the fact that his partner Gerry Queen was too similar a type of player, and neither of them had the muscle to cause problems to hefty First Division defences.

Gerry Queen was signed from Kilmarnock by Bert Head, who said of him; "When I weigh up a player I look for just 8 attributes...Gerry has 7, which shows how highly I rate him." He only averaged a goal every four games for Palace, and was unfortunate that he never had a good target man to feed off, ending his Palace days scampering around looking for scraps up front with Willie Wallace. Queen had the distinction of scoring in Palace's first ever game in the First Division, against Manchester United, and it was his goal that beat Liverpool in 1971, Palace's only league victory over that team to date. The goal which I always remember, though, was in the Boxing Day game against Chelsea in 1970, when Palace were hammered 5-1, but Queen looped a long-range, wind-assisted googly past Peter 'The Cat' Bonetti

from an implausible distance, to briefly give Palace the lead.

Willie Wallace was one of Bert Head's least successful Scottish buys, and both **Derek Possee** and **Alan Whittle** had far bigger reputations than were warranted before they came to Palace. Whittle at least scored one terrific goal on his debut against Manchester United, and won a few penalties, but Possee simply wasn't the same player who had been so good at Millwall, and the two of them together up front were a dead loss, not just because they were so short.

After Swindlehurst had established himself in the team, he had a variety of striking partners, the most of effective of whom were the heroic **Jeff Bourne** and the unlucky **Mike Elwiss**, and **Dave Kemp** had his moments, but Swindlehurst was undoubtedly at his best when playing alongside **Ian Walsh**. Walsh was from the vintage crop of youth team players that served Venables so well at the end of the 1970s, and he was a perfect foil to the big man, although never a great goalscorer. He was a very busy player, always looking for the ball in deep and wide positions, and for a small man he was pretty good in the air, notably when scoring the first goal against Burnley in the 1979 promotion clincher. Palace's success helped him to win a place in the Welsh national team, but Venables regrettably preferred to play his expensive signing **Mike Flanagan** in his place, and Walsh's appearances from then on were only intermittent, although he came in and out of the side for a couple of years before Steve Kember released him to Swansea.

Flanagan himself was a ponderous player who I for one never took to, and **Tony Sealey** was no better or worse, and it wasn't until **Kevin Mabbutt** signed from Bristol City in 1981 that Palace at last had a good forward, although he had to try his best with scant assistance from either Tommy Langley or Chris Jones. It is a great shame when you see a good player unable to exploit his talent because of injury, but Mabbutt was clearly fated never to make it to the top of his profession, Palace finally losing patience with him in 1984 after several false dawns.

When Steve Coppell took over in 1984, he experimented with several partners for Trevor Aylott – Andy Gray and Phil Barber both having some success – but once the green but talented **Ian Wright** had found his feet there was no looking back. In his first season Wright scored some important goals after coming on as substitute, but his second year was a bit of a disappointment, with only nine goals from 42

IAN WRIGHT

starts, the usual kind of percentage for a Palace forward until then. After Mark Bright had been installed, though, Wright suddenly found a new confidence and began to play with abandon, and it was soon evident that here was one of the most naturally skilful players unearthed for many years, not just at Palace, but in the English game. His haul of goals from then on tells part of the story, and there is no more delightful sight than Ian Wright pouncing on to a loose ball and lashing it into the net, but there is so much more to his game than that. He can devastate defences with a wicked burst of speed, but his most enjoyable trick is when he brings down a high ball with

his back to the goal, and with one neat flick controls it, turns past the centre back and leaves him sprawling in his wake as he bears down on the goalkeeper. As well as being brilliant with the ball at his feet, Wright is a deadly header of the ball – although shorter than sometimes claimed – and as mild mannered a personality as you could wish to meet. In short, I think he's wonderful. His first season in Division One was a frustrating one, with his leg being broken on two separate occasions, but I have no doubt that he has the ability, given a bit of luck, to prove himself in the near future as a world-class player, England's answer to Toto Schillaci. Such a prospect should thrill anyone who saw him come on as substitute and score two spectacular goals in the F.A.Cup final, which put Palace to within seven minutes of winning the Cup. His first goal that day was something extra special, and deserves to be remembered as one of the great Cup Final goals of all time.

No other player even comes close to challenging Ian Wright for his place in my imaginary team, but although the obvious choice as his partner would be Mark Bright – who is himself still underrated – I shall choose Dave Swindlehurst as my No.9, a player who performed in three divisions for Palace, and whose true worth wasn't properly appreciated until long after he had gone.

Postscript

An essential quality for a Palace fan is optimism, and I find myself looking forward to the new season with higher hopes than ever before, believing above all in Steve Coppell's ability to continue to improve the side. Having stayed up a shade comfortably, he knows too much to become complacent, and has already made two excellent purchases in Glyn Hodges and John Humphrey, strengthening two of the weaker positions. I say that with all due respect and affection for Phil Barber and John Pemberton, but to stay in Division One, let alone to challenge for honours, Palace must buy better quality players wherever possible. Both Hodges and Humphrey happen to be players who I have wished were on our side before, and if there are no more changes made before the new season, it is still an exciting prospect. However, it still seems that Coppell wants to buy a top class centre half, and if he manages that then I truly believe that Palace can become established as one of the top teams in the First Division; but then I have said that before.

For half a season in 1979, Terry Venables appeared to have built a team capable of living with the best, but they plummetted into oblivion only the following year. Bert Head's team had a similarly brief spell of success in 1970, only to decline rapidly over the next couple of seasons and land in the Third Division. The evidence of Palace's past attempts at storming the First Division suggests that the second season after promotion is the crucial one, and what happens in the year to come could make or break Palace for the foreseeable future.

Logically, the new staff should bring improved results, but I anticipate that the vital question will be whether the midfield axis of Geoff Thomas and Andy Gray can fulfil the potential that they have shown in the past, and set up a productive combination with Bright and Wright up front. I think that they can, and that Palace will finish in the top six before winning the F.A.Cup.

See you at Wembley.

Chris Winter
August 1990
South East London